ESSENTIALS

of Knowledge Management

Bryan Bergeron

WILEY

John Wiley & Sons, Inc.

For general information on our other products and services, or technical support,
please contact our Customer Care Department within the United States at
800-762-2974, outside the United States at 317-572-3993, or fax 317-572-4002.

Wiley also publishes its books in a variety of electronic formats. Some content
that appears in print may not be available in electronic books.

For more information about Wiley products, visit our web site at *www.wiley.com*.

Library of Congress Cataloging-in-Publication Data

Bergeron, Bryan P.
    Essentials of knowledge management / Bryan Bergeron.
        p. cm. -- (Essentials series)
    Includes index.
    ISBN 0-471-28113-1 (pbk. : alk. paper)
    1. Knowledge management. I. Title. II. Series.
HD30.2 .B463 2003
658.4'038--dc21   2002155501

Printed in the United States of America.

10 9 8 7 6 5 4 3 2 1

To Miriam Goodman

Contents

Preface

Essentials of Knowledge Management is a practical survey of the field of Knowledge Management (KM)—a business optimization strategy that identifies, selects, organizes, distills, and packages information essential to the business of the company in a way that improves employee performance and corporate competitiveness. The preservation and packaging of corporate knowledge (i.e., information in the context in which it is used) is especially relevant today, given that the majority of the service-oriented workforce is composed of knowledge workers. To compete successfully in today's economy, organizations have to treat the knowledge that contributes to their core competencies just as they would any other strategic, irreplaceable asset.

The aim of this book is to examine approaches to Knowledge Management that contribute to corporate competitiveness, and those that don't. The book assumes an intelligent CEO-level reader, but one who is unfamiliar with the nuances of the KM field and needs to come up to speed in one quick reading. After completing this book, readers will understand how their business can be optimized using KM techniques and strategies. Moreover, readers will be able to converse comfortably with KM professionals, understand what to look for when hiring KM staff and consultants, and understand the investment and likely returns on various KM approaches. To illustrate the practical, business aspects of Knowledge Management in an easily digestible fashion, each chapter contains a vignette that deals with key technical, cultural, or economic issues of the technology.

Reader Return on Investment

After reading the following chapters, the reader will be able to:

- Understand Knowledge Management from historical, economic, technical, and corporate culture perspectives, including what KM is and isn't.

- Have a working vocabulary of the field of Knowledge Management and be able to communicate intelligently with KM professionals and vendors.

- Understand the trade-offs between the commercial options available for a KM implementation.

- Understand the significance of Knowledge Management on the company's bottom line.

- Understand the relationship between Knowledge Management and other business optimization strategies.

- Understand how KM professionals work and think.

- Have a set of specific recommendations that can be used to establish and manage a KM effort.

- Understand the technologies, including their trade-offs, that can be used to implement Knowledge Management in the corporation.

- Appreciate best practices—what works, why it works, and how to recognize a successful KM effort.

Organization of This Book

This book is organized into modular topics related to Knowledge Management. It is divided into eight chapters.

Chapter 1: Overview

The first chapter provides an overview of the key concepts, terminology, and the historical context of practical Knowledge Management in the workplace. It illustrates, for example, how every successful organization uses Knowledge Management to some degree, albeit perhaps not in a sophisticated, formalized way. This chapter also differentiates between knowledge as an organizational process versus simply a collection of data that can be stored in a database.

Chapter 2: Knowledge Organizations

Taking the perspective of the corporate senior management, this chapter explores the implications of embracing Knowledge Management as an organizational theme. It explores the role of chief executive as chief knowledge officer, how any KM initiative is primarily one of corporate culture change, what can be expected through application of KM strategies in a large organization, general classes of KM initiatives—including gaining knowledge from customers, creating new revenues from existing knowledge, and capturing individual's tacit knowledge for reuse—as well as a review of the predictors of a successful initiative.

Chapter 3: Knowledge Workers

This chapter explores Knowledge Management from the employees' perspective. Topics include dealing with employee resistance to the increased overhead of not only performing their jobs but taking time to document their behavior for others, addressing the potential reward for a job well done with decreased job security, the importance of creating employee recognition and reward systems to encouraging employee participation in a KM initiative, and ways to use KM techniques to enhance employee effectiveness.

Chapter 4: Process

This chapter focuses on Knowledge Management as a process. Topics include process reengineering, competency measurement, how to best apply collaborative systems, approaches to unobtrusive knowledge capture, filtering and refining knowledge, methodologies for applying knowledge for decision support, and how Knowledge Management relates to traditional business processes and business models.

Chapter 5: Technology

This chapter explores the many computer and communications technologies that can be used to enhance the organizational and behavioral aspects of a Knowledge Management initiative. Included are a survey of technologies for knowledge collection (e.g., data mining, text summarizing, the use of intelligent agents, and a variety of information retrieval methodologies), knowledge storage and retrieval (e.g., knowledge bases and information repositories), and knowledge dissemination and application (e.g., intranets and internets, groupware, decision support tools, and collaborative systems).

Chapter 6: Solutions

This chapter looks at the various solutions offered by vendors in the Knowledge Management market. Topics include defining assessment metrics of performance, industry standards and best practices, and how to assess the impact of a KM initiative on qualitative factors surrounding organization-wide change of corporate vision, values, and behaviors.

Chapter 7: Economics

This chapter explores the financial aspects of Knowledge Management, from a return-on-investment perspective. Topics include pricing models for information infrastructure development, overhead costs, contractual issues, and hidden costs of Knowledge Management, and how to justify the cost of investing in new technologies. The chapter also explores the knowledge economy in terms of the knowledge value chain.

Chapter 8: Getting There

The final chapter provides some concrete examples of the resources, time, and costs involved in embarking on a practical Knowledge Management effort. Topics include implementation challenges, working with vendors, achieving employee buy-in, including how to shift corporate culture from knowledge sequestering to knowledge sharing, employee education, realistic implementation timelines, and managing risk. The chapter ends with a look to the future of Knowledge Management as it relates to information technology, process, and organizational change.

Further Reading

This section lists some of the more relevant works in the area of Knowledge Management, at a level appropriate to a chief executive or upper-level manager.

Glossary

The glossary contains words defined throughout the text as well the most common terms a reader will encounter in the Knowledge Management literature.

How to Use This Book

For those new to Knowledge Management, the best way to tackle the subject is simply to read each chapter in order; however, because each chapter is written as a stand-alone module, readers interested in, for example, the economics of Knowledge Management can go directly to Chapter 7, "Economics."

Throughout the book, "In the Real World" sections provide real-world examples of how Knowledge Management is being used to improve corporate competitiveness and ability to adapt to change. Similarly, a "Tips & Techniques" section in each chapter offers concrete steps that the reader can take to benefit from a KM initiative. Key terms are defined in the glossary. In addition, readers who want to delve deeper into the business, technical, or corporate culture aspects of Knowledge Management are encouraged to consult the list of books and publications provided in the Further Reading section.

Acknowledgments

I would like to thank my enduring editorial associate, Miriam Goodman, for her assistance in creating this work. In addition, special thanks are in order to my editor at John Wiley & Sons, Sheck Cho, for his insight and encouragement.

CHAPTER 1

Overview

Readers prepared to add a powerful new tool to their arsenal of competitive business strategies may be surprised to discover that Knowledge Management (KM) has more to do with ancient civilizations than with some recent innovation in information technology (IT). Consider that, since antiquity, organized business has sought a competitive advantage that would allow it to serve customers as efficiently as possible, maximize profits, develop a loyal customer following, and keep the competition at bay, regardless of whether the product is rugs, spices, or semiconductors. Beginning about 15,000 years ago, this advantage was writing down the selected knowledge of merchants, artisans, physicians, and government administrators for future reference. Writing was used to create enduring records of the society's rules, regulations, and cumulative knowledge, including who owed and paid money to the largest enterprise of the time—the government.

In Mesopotamia about 5,000 years ago, people began to lose track of the thousands of baked-clay tablets used to record legal contracts, tax assessments, sales, and law. The solution was the start of the first institution dedicated to Knowledge Management, the library. In libraries, located in the center of town, the collection of tablets was attended to by professional knowledge managers. An unfortunate side effect of this concentration of information was that libraries made convenient targets for military conquest.

Even though war had the effect of spreading writings and drawings to new cultures, access to the information they contained was largely restricted to political and religious leaders. Such leaders represented the elite class, who either understood the language in which the scrolls or tablets were written or could afford to have the works translated into their native tongue. Things improved for the public in the West a little over five centuries ago, with the invention of movable type and the printing press. With the Renaissance and prosperity came a literate class and the practice of printing in the common tongue instead of in Latin.

In the world of commerce, the expertise of many professions continued to be passed on through apprenticeship, sometimes supplemented by books and other forms of collective memory. This concentration of knowledge limited actual manufacturing to relatively small shops in which skilled craftsmen toiled over piecework. Things changed with the introduction of the assembly line as a method of production. The industrial revolution was possible largely because rows of machines—not an oral or written tradition—provided the structural memory of the process involved in the production of guns, fabrics, machinery, and other goods whose design enabled mass production. No longer was a lengthy apprenticeship, or literacy, or even an understanding of the manufacturing process required for someone to quickly achieve acceptable performance at a task. Anyone, including women and children with no education, could learn to refill a bobbin with yarn, keep a parts bin filled, or operate a machine in a few hours—and keep at it for 12 hours at a time, seven days a week. For the first time, productivity could be measured, benchmarks or standards could be established, and processes could be optimized. As a result, productivity increased, goods became more plentiful, and they could be offered to the masses at an affordable price while maintaining a healthy profit margin for the company and its investors. However, knowledge of the overall process and how individual workers contributed to the whole was closely held by a handful of assembly-line designers and senior management.

Modern business in the postindustrial U.S. service economy is largely a carryover from this manufacturing tradition, especially as it relates to accounting practices and corporate valuation. For example, the government, a silent partner in every business venture, recognizes the purchase price and depreciation schedule of physical assets, but not the processes or knowledge held in the minds of workers. Similarly, the manner in which employees are assigned positions in the modern corporation reflects the industrial era in which individual workers have little knowledge of—or voice in—the overall business model. It's common, for example, for large rooms crammed with cubicles to house hundreds of workers who mindlessly process printed or electronic documents. These workers manipulate and validate data, according to easily learned rules established by management. As a result, the knowledge of the overall process resides in the minds of senior management, and employees for the most part are treated as if they were easily replaceable assembly-line workers in a manufacturing plant.

At higher levels of the knowledge worker hierarchy, university degrees and certificates from various organizations or guilds provide the self-imposed labels that managers and professionals use to qualify for one of the predefined positions in the matrix of the organization. These knowledge workers have more of an overall picture of the business than lower-level front-line workers do, but there is likely duplication of mistakes in different departments since these workers may not have a process in place to share knowledge of best practices. For example, professionals in multiple departments with the organization may be experimenting with outsourcing, each discovering independently that the promised savings are far less that the popular business press suggests.

Despite the parallels in front-line employees working with data instead of textiles or iron, the reality of the modern corporate workplace also contrasts sharply with what was considered by employees and management as a permanent condition until only a few decades ago. The situation of lifetime employment offered by large manufacturing plants in the steel, petroleum, and automobile industries during the latter half of the twentieth century is virtually unheard of today, even with labor unions. Given the volatility of the economy and mobility of the workforce, new entrants into the workforce can expect to work with five or more firms during their lifetimes. Even in Japan, where lifetime employment was once an unwritten rule, major corporations routinely downsize thousands of workers at a time.

While industrialization may have been detrimental to the environment and some social institutions, it isn't responsible for the current pressure on businesses to be more competitive. Rather, economic volatility, high employee turnover, international shifts in political power, global competition, and rapid change characterize the modern economic environment. As a result, the modern business organization can't compete effectively in the marketplace without skilled managers and employees and without methods for managing their knowledge of people, and all the processes and technologies involved in the business, including information technology.

EXHIBIT 1.1

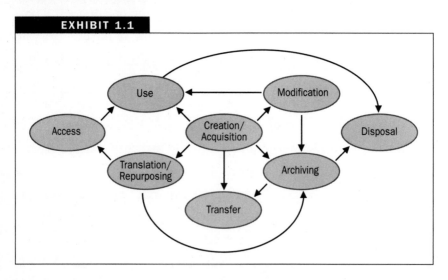

Managing information throughout the ages, whether expressed in the form of figures cut into clay tablets, rows of machines on a factory floor, or a roomful of cubicles in which service providers handle electronic documents, entails a web of eight interrelated processes (see Exhibit 1.1). Consider the eight processes in the context of a multimedia production company:

1. *Creation/acquisition.* The multimedia—some combination of images, video, and sound—is either authored from scratch or acquired by some means. For example, the multimedia company many create a series of images depicting a new manufacturing process for a client.

2. *Modification.* The multimedia is modified to suit the immediate needs of the client. For example, the raw multimedia may be reformatted for use in a glossy brochure.

3. *Use.* The information is employed for some useful purpose, which may include being sold and distributed. For example, the brochure is printed for distribution by the client.

4. *Archiving.* The information is stored in a form and format that will survive the elements and time, from the perspectives of both physical and cultural change. The multimedia included in the brochure may be burned onto a CD-ROM and stored in a fireproof safe off site, for example.

5. *Transfer.* The information is transferred from one place to another. The electronic files of the brochure may be distributed via the Internet to clients in corporate offices around the globe.

6. *Translation/repurposing.* The information is translated into a form more useful for a second group of users or for a new purpose. The images used in the brochure are translated into web-

compatible images to create an online brochure on the client's intranet web site.

7. *Access.* Limited access to the translated or original information is provided to users as a function of their position or role in the organization. For example, managers in the client's organization with the access codes and passwords to the password-protected web site can view the online brochure that describes the new manufacturing process.

8. *Disposal.* Information with no future value is discarded to save space and reduce overhead. When multimedia for a second brochure is created by the multimedia company, the files relating to the online and printed brochures are purged from the electronic system. However, printed and CD-ROM copies of the information are saved for reference or for the historical record.

In addition to these individual steps, there is an underlying process for tracking the information in the system. For example, it's possible for the original information to be archived while a modified version is being translated for another purpose.

Given this historical perspective on information, society, and business, let's begin the exploration of contemporary Knowledge Management with a definition, a review of KM principles, and a vignette to illustrate the concepts as they apply to business.

Definition

The Holy Grail of Knowledge Management is the ability to selectively capture, archive, and access the best practices of work-related knowledge and decision making from employees and managers for both individual and group behaviors. For example, a manager may have knowledge of how to quickly procure parts from a supplier (individual behavior) as

Knowledge Management in the Field

One of the pioneers in the modern business knowledge management arena is the American Productivity and Quality Center (APQC). For several decades prior to APQC's 1995 Knowledge Management Symposium, held in conjunction with Arthur Andersen Companies, most KM work was conducted in academic laboratories. Much of this work was performed in specific areas. For example, throughout the 1980s, research in Knowledge Management in medicine was carried out in the Decision Systems Group at Harvard Medical School, with funding from the National Library of Medicine.

Today, many of the Fortune 1000 companies have ongoing KM projects aimed at general and specific business functions. A partial list of these companies includes:

Air Products & Chemicals Inc.

Allstate Insurance Company

Army Medical Department

Bank of America

Best Buy

BHP Billiton

ChevronTexaco

Corning Inc.

Deere & Co.

Dell Computer

Department of National Defense, Canada

Intel Corp.

Northrop Grumman

Raytheon Company

Schlumberger Oilfield Services

Shell E&P

Siemens AG

Union Pacific Railroad Company

U.S. Census Bureau

U.S. Department of the Navy—Acquisition Reform Office

U.S. Department of Veterans Affairs

U.S. General Services Administration

U.S. National Security Agency

U.S. Naval Sea Systems Command

U.S. Social Security Administration

World Bank

Xerox

Xerox Connect

(continues)

well as how to work with other managers in getting policies pushed through the corporate hierarchy (group behavior).

In practice, most KM practices fall short of this ideal. This is primarily because it's virtually impossible to capture the thoughts, beliefs, and behaviors of a manager or employee in a way that is both economical and complete enough to provide another person—or machine—with enough quality information to make the same decisions, exhibit the same leadership principles, or perform the same complex tasks at the same level of performance. One of the first challenges in understanding exactly what practical Knowledge Management involves is agreeing on a definition. Part of the confusion arises because of how the term "Knowledge Management" is used by vendors who sell products that have very little to do with the ideal and more to do with relabeling products initially directed at other markets. There is also confusion caused by terminology borrowed from the academic community regarding the use of knowledge in artificial intelligence research, much of which doesn't apply to Knowledge Management.

This book defines Knowledge Management from a practical business perspective.

Knowledge Management (KM) is a deliberate, systematic business optimization strategy that selects, distills, stores, organizes, packages, and communicates information essential to the business of a company in a manner that improves employee performance and corporate competitiveness.

From this definition, it should be clear that Knowledge Management is fundamentally about a systematic approach to managing intellectual assets and other information in a way that provides the company with a competitive advantage. Knowledge Management is a business optimization strategy, and not limited to a particular technology or source of information. In most cases, a wide variety of information technologies play a key role in a KM initiative, simply because of the savings in time and effort they provide over manual operations.

Knowledge Management is agnostic when it comes to the type and source of information, which can range from the mathematical description of the inner workings of a machine to a document that describes the process used by a customer support representative to escalate customer complaints within the business organization. Consider the example of the legal firm, whose senior partners create written templates (the information) for ease of creating specific documents. Such a firm has a KM system that can vastly increase its productivity. If the templates are moved to a word processing system, then the ease of creating a new legal document may be enhanced by several orders of magnitude.

As another example, consider a small business owner who moves her bookkeeping from bound journals to a computerized system. Unlike the paper-based system, the electronic system can show, at a glance, the percentage of revenue spent on advertising and revenue relative to the same period last year—all in intuitive business graphics.

A marketing and communications company that takes all copy and images that have been used in previous advertising campaigns and digitizes them so that they can be stored on CD-ROM instead of in a filing cabinet isn't in itself practicing Knowledge Management. However, if the company takes the digitized data and indexes them with a software program that allows someone to search for specific content instead of manually paging through hundreds of screens, it is practicing Knowledge Management.

Given the range of business activities that can be considered examples of Knowledge Management, one of the most confusing aspects of the practice is clarifying exactly what constitutes knowledge, information, and data. Although the academic community has spent decades debating the issue, for our purposes, these definitions and concepts apply:

- *Data* are numbers. They are numerical quantities or other attributes derived from observation, experiment, or calculation.

- *Information* is data in context. Information is a collection of data and associated explanations, interpretations, and other textual material concerning a particular object, event, or process.

- *Metadata* is data about information. Metadata includes descriptive summaries and high-level categorization of data and information. That is, metadata is information about the context in which information is used.

- *Knowledge* is information that is organized, synthesized, or summarized to enhance comprehension, awareness, or understanding. That is, knowledge is a combination of metadata and an awareness of the context in which the metadata can be applied successfully.

- *Instrumental understanding* is the clear and complete idea of the nature, significance, or explanation of something. It is a personal, internal power to render experience intelligible by relating specific knowledge to broad concepts.

As shown in Exhibit 1.2, the concepts defining knowledge are related hierarchically, with data at the bottom of the hierarchy and under-

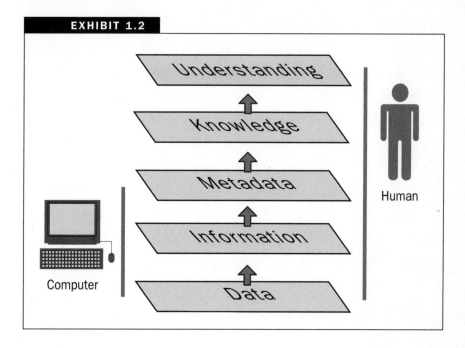

EXHIBIT 1.2

Understanding

Knowledge

Metadata

Information

Data

Human

Computer

standing at the top. In general, each level up the hierarchy involves greater contextual richness. For example, in medicine, the hierarchy could appear as:

- *Data*. Patient Temperature: 102° F; Pulse: 109 beats per minute; Age: 75.

- *Information*. "Fever" is a temperature greater than 100° F; "tachycardia" is a pulse greater than 100 beats per minute; "elderly" is someone with an age greater than 75.

- *Metadata*. The combination of fever and tachycardia in the elderly can be life threatening.

- *Knowledge*. The patient probably has a serious case of the flu.

- *Instrumental understanding*. The patient should be admitted to the hospital ASAP and treated for the flu.

In this example, data are the individual measurements of temperature, pulse, and patient age, which have no real meaning out of context.

However, when related to the range of normal measurements (information), the patient is seen in the context of someone who is elderly with a temperature and tachycardia. In the greater context of healthcare (metadata), the combination of findings is viewed as life threatening. A clinician who has seen this pattern of patient presentation in the past diagnoses the patient as having the flu (knowledge). In addition, given the patient's age and condition, the clinician determines (understanding) that the patient should be admitted to the hospital and treated for the flu.

Taking an example from a sales agent working for a life insurance company, the knowledge hierarchy associated with a potential customer of a life insurance policy could read as:

- *Data*. Marital status: Single; Annual Income: $32,000; Age: 25.
- *Information*. Death risk is greater for single males than married males; median income is an annual income greater than $19,000; and "young adult" applies to age less than 25.
- *Metadata*. The prospect represents a moderate to low risk.
- *Knowledge*. Given that the prospect has no dependents, insurance has no value to him unless the policy can be used as an investment vehicle.
- *Instrumental understanding*. The prospect should be sold a $100,000 cash value life insurance policy.

In both examples, more than simply grouping data or information is involved in moving up the hierarchy. Rather, there are rules of thumb or heuristics that provide contextual information. In the case of life insurance, the heuristics for risk assignment might be:

- *Low risk*. Age less than 28, marital status single or married.
- *Moderate risk*. Age 28 to 54, marital status married.
- *High risk*. Age 55 or greater, marital status single or married.

As these risk heuristics illustrate, a challenge in creating heuristics is guaranteeing completeness and gracefully handling exceptions. In this case, there is no classification for a 30-year-old single applicant. Similarly, should a 55-year-old marathon runner be considered in the same high-risk category as a 75-year-old overweight smoker?

The example also illustrates the contribution of beliefs to knowledge, in that knowledge can be thought of as facts, heuristics, and beliefs. For example, there may be no basis for assigning married prospects to the moderate risk category other than hearsay that married men may live longer than single men. Similarly, in business, there exist beliefs and prejudices that may or may not be based in reality but nonetheless affect business decisions. Since these beliefs may be associated with beneficial outcomes, it's important somehow to incorporate beliefs in the concept of business knowledge.

Although the concept of knowledge is roughly equivalent to that of metadata, unlike data, information, or metadata, knowledge incorporates awareness—a trait that implies a human, rather than a computer, host. Although artificial intelligence (AI) systems may one day be capable of awareness and perhaps even understanding, the current state of technology limits computers to the metadata level. Even though the concept of Knowledge Management probably would be better labeled Metadata Management, the latter term is unwieldy and potentially more confusing than simply referring to the concept of Metadata Management as Knowledge Management.

Returning to the wording in the definition of Knowledge Management offered earlier, it is important to note that the process is selective, in that only the important facts and contextual information is saved. Some sort of filter mechanism must be in place to avoid collecting a massive amount of information that is too expensive to store and can't be easily searched or retrieved efficiently.

Similarly, the KM process involves distillation of data to information and of information to knowledge. This step further clarifies and limits the amount of data that must be stored. Before the information can be stored in some type of memory system, however, it has to be organized in a way that facilitates later retrieval. Organization usually involves deciding on a representation language and a vocabulary to identify concepts. For example, in the risk assignment for insurance policy prospects, does the designation "single" apply to recently divorced prospects as well? Furthermore, the concept of Low Risk can be represented mathematically, as in:

$$LR = AGE < 28 \text{ AND } MS = SINGLE \text{ OR } MS = MARRIED$$

Or in simple text prose:

Low Risk is assigned to prospective customers less than 28 years of age who are married or single.

Storage is most often accomplished using several forms of information technology, typically including PCs and servers running database management software. However, data sitting in a repository is of no value unless it's put to use. As such, Knowledge Management is a two-way process, in that data are first captured, manipulated, and stored, and then the resulting information is packaged or reformatted to suit the needs of the user. As an example of this packaging, consider the example of risk assignment for insurance prospects. The original materials and process description may be reformatted as a graphical decision tree, as in Exhibit 1.3.

Similarly, the text originally generated by managers may be simplified in both organization and vocabulary for easier access by line workers. For

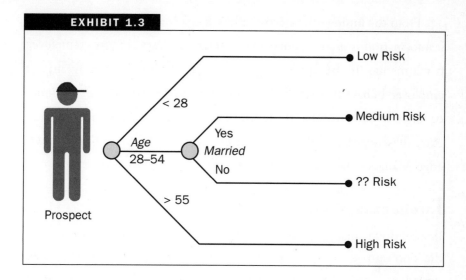

EXHIBIT 1.3

example, an engineering white paper on calibrating a computer monitor might state:

> The display's gamma should be adjusted to match the Pantone 145. . . .

However, a customer support representative who has to walk customers through the calibration process is more likely to understand—and be able to communicate to the customer—something like this:

> The display's color display curve (see photo) should be adjusted so that the color displayed on the monitor is as close to the supplied color patch as possible. . .

This packaging, or formatting, of information in a form most intelligible for its intended consumer can be performed semiautomatically with software tools such as synonym generators, or manually through an editorial review process. Finally, for the information to be useful, it has to be communicated to the intended recipient. Having a wealth of process and factual data in a sophisticated but dormant information system is like having a massive book library and not using it.

From the business perspective, Knowledge Management is useful only if information is used in a directed manner, such as to improve employee performance. If the information is useful, it should directly impact employee behavior and be reflected in increased efficiency, effectiveness, or diligence. Ultimately, the improvement in corporate competitiveness from the corporate perspective is the rationale for investing in Knowledge Management.

Intellectual Capital

In traditional management of early twentieth century that dealt with the optimum utilization of labor, parts, and other physical resources, capital was considered limited to the factories, machines, and other human-made inputs into the production process. In the modern corporation with a KM initiative, the concept of capital is extended to include ephemeral intellectual capital and its impact on individual and organizational behavior. Although intellectual capital can be lumped

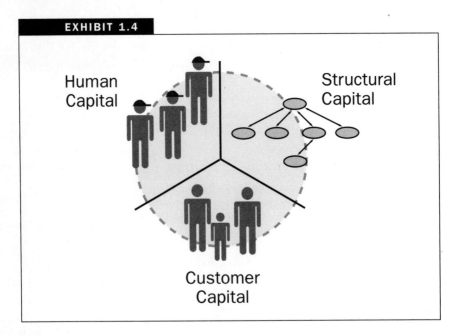

EXHIBIT 1.4

Human Capital

Structural Capital

Customer Capital

into one concept, from a KM perspective, it's more useful to consider the constituent components individually, as shown in Exhibit 1.4.

The three major components of intellectual capital are:

1. *Human capital.* The knowledge, skills, and competencies of the people in the organization. Human capital is owned by the employees and managers that possess it. Without a KM system in place, when employees and managers leave the company, they take their skills, competencies, and knowledge with them.

2. *Customer capital.* The value of the organization's relationships with its customers, including customer loyalty, distribution channels, brands, licensing, and franchises. Because customers often form bonds with a salesperson or customer representative, customer capital typically is jointly owned by employee and employer. The proportion of customer capital held by employees and employers depends on the relative contribution of customer loyalty to customer capital.

3. *Structural capital.* The process, structures, information systems, and intellectual properties that are independent of the employees and managers who created them. Intellectual properties are sometimes considered as a separate, fourth component of intellectual capital.

Each of the three major components of intellectual capital can be subdivided into finer levels of granularity, as shown in Exhibit 1.5. For example, for KM purposes, Human Capital is composed of three kinds of knowledge: tacit, implicit, and explicit knowledge.

Tacit knowledge is knowledge that is ingrained at a subconscious level and therefore difficult to explain to others. An expert machinist may be extremely skilled at operating a particular machine, for example, but be unable to instruct an apprentice on exactly how to duplicate his expertise. Most knowledge involving pattern recognition skills fall under the category of tacit knowledge. For example, a seasoned radiologist can generally look at a typical radiographic film of a patient's chest and instantly decide if the film is normal or abnormal. However, eliciting the process that the expert diagnostician used to make her determination is virtually impossible. When forced to teach residents and students how to read radiographic studies, radiologists use a systematic approach, looking at bones first, then soft tissues, and so on, so that the learner has a place to start in the learning process. In fact, however, the system most radiologists teach isn't the system that they use. Similarly, pathologists, like master chess players, use one system and teach another.

Implicit knowledge, like tacit knowledge, typically is controlled by experts. However, unlike tacit knowledge, implicit knowledge can be extracted from the expert—through a process termed knowledge engineering. For example, an expert at assigning risk to insurance prospects might use the risk heuristics discussed earlier, assigning risk as a function of age and marital status. Once a new employee is given the same heuristics, either in the form of a set of rules or drawn as a decision tree, he or she can make a risk assignment with the same level of accuracy as the expert, who may have developed the heuristic through years of experience.

The third form of knowledge, explicit knowledge, can easily be conveyed from someone proficient at a task to someone else through written or verbal communications. The recipe for a cake, the steps involved in bolting a car door to the main chassis on an assembly line, and the list of ingredients required for a chemical process are all explicit knowledge. Unlike tacit and implicit knowledge, explicit knowledge often can be found in a book or operating manual.

EXHIBIT 1.5

Intellectual Capital Components

Human
Attitude
Competencies
Education
Knowledge
Skills

Customer
Brand
Company name
Customers
Distribution channels
Franchise agreements
License agreements
Loyalty

Structural
Copyright
Corporate culture
Design rights
Financial relations
Information technology infrastructure
Management processes
Service marks
Trade secrets
Trademarks

Since management in every organization manipulates human, structural, and customer capital, every organization uses Knowledge Management to some degree, though not necessarily in a sophisticated, formalized way. Not only does the relative percentage of the three types of intellectual capital vary from one company to the next, but the percent of human, customer, and structural capital varies from company to company, as well.

The following vignette illustrates the practical value of a formalized KM approach in increasing corporate competitiveness.

Tale of Two Companies

Two companies at opposite ends of the country, Healthcare Productions in San Francisco and Medical Multimedia in Boston, are involved in supporting the pharmaceutical industry. Both companies create promotional materials for conferences, educational programs for clinicians, and web sites for disseminating prescribing information about drugs to healthcare providers.

Medical Multimedia, in operation for about five years, has 35 employees and has been operating at a modest profit margin for the past three years. About half of the employees are involved in creating and manipulating images, sounds, videos, and other multimedia assets, while the remainder are concerned with programming, marketing, sales, and customer support. With two new contracts in the works, and the company already at capacity due to ongoing projects, Ron, the head of multimedia production, is operating in panic mode. Multimedia content has always been created for particular projects; when the project was delivered, the assets were stored in an ad hoc manner on various company servers, CDs, and hard drives. The content that was burned onto CD-ROMs has been stored in a fireproof safe in Ron's office.

With the deadlines for the two new contracts looming, there is no time for anyone to excavate for the content previously developed— some of which could be repurposed for the new contracts. Yet there is insufficient time to redraw the figures, synthesize the sounds, and render the video images from scratch. Faced with this reality, Ron approaches the president of the company and requests permission to hire a multimedia consultant immediately.

The president agrees, and Mary, a multimedia consultant with over 20 years experience in the field, is brought on board the next week. Mary suggests that Ron use a multimedia database program specially designed to keep track of graphics, sounds, and pictures, and their associated intellectual property status, so that components of Medical Multimedia's holdings can be quickly and easily repurposed.

With the go-ahead from Ron, Mary lays the groundwork for the multimedia database program by interviewing everyone who eventually will directly or indirectly use the system, including:

- *Artists.* Graphic, video, and sound artists who need to reference prior work or continue work on active projects.

- *Corporate Counsel.* To verify intellectual property status of individual work. Some images and sounds held by Medical Multimedia are licensed from third parties for specific purposes or numbers of users, whereas others are created in house. A graphic originally licensed for a print publication may need to be relicensed for use on the web.

- *Management.* Ron and those involved in project management need to frequently assess the progress of graphic artists and verify that production schedules are on track.

- *Programmers.* The programming staff needs some way to assess the technical challenges associated with each media asset destined to be incorporated in electronic products. For example, some sounds and images may need to be converted into a form that is compatible with the web.

Not interviewed but considered in the design of the system are:

- *Customers.* Media typically needs to be exported periodically to customers for their sign-off before the sounds and graphics are incorporated into the brochures, books, or electronic products.

- *Potential Clients.* Potential clients who are interested in the style and quality of artwork may pay the company a site visit prior to signing a contract for deliverables.
- *Marketing and Sales.* This group uses the media in presentations to customers and potential customers

In the interview process, Mary is concerned not only with the overall process of use but also with exactly how the assets will be cataloged and then retrieved. For example, she establishes a standard file-naming scheme that guarantees unique file names. In addition, she creates a database structure that incorporates the needs of artists, management, programmers, and corporate counsel that includes:

- *Artist/Licensor.* Name of the creator.
- *Copyright Holder.* The copyright holder of the multimedia.
- *Creation Date.* The date the media was created or acquired.
- *Creation Tool/Version.* Name and version of the software used to create the asset.
- *File Name.* The full name of the media file, as it appears on the computer.
- *Index Terms.* Standardized names used to classify the media, in this case using a vocabulary developed by the National Library of Medicine for its multimedia holdings.
- *License Expiration Date.* If licensed, the date of expiration.
- *License Restrictions.* For acquired multimedia, the restrictions imposed by the supplier.
- *Physical Location.* Where the actual multimedia resides in the company's information system.
- *Project.* Name of the project the media is intended to support.
- *Source File.* For media rendered from models or other sources, the name of the source file.

- *Version*. Version of the file. In the course of editing an image for production, a dozen or more versions may be created, for example.

During Mary's work, she discovers that management has lost touch with its multimedia assets and its intellectual capital. Other than the person directly involved in managing or creating specific multimedia, no one knows the specific processes involved in creating products for market. Management is so focused on company growth through capturing new contracts that existing processes are being ignored.

For example, one of the company's core competencies, the ability to render realistic, three-dimensional (3-D) images of patients, is dependent on one artist who is fluent in a custom software package that is so specialized and complex that it takes months to master. Furthermore, unbeknownst to upper management, Ron has been unable to locate anyone to hire full time to assist the artist. The best that Ron can do is to identify a freelance consultant in Seattle and one in Oakland to handle some of the work. If the in-house artist were to leave, the entire production work of the company would come to a halt.

Since Medical Multimedia specializes in custom work, most of the internal processes parallel those of the artist, in that they are highly person-dependent and only the creator knows exactly how he performs his work. Realizing the potential for disaster, Mary approached the president of the company and suggested that she expand her multimedia asset management project to include the company's intellectual capital. Given her success with the multimedia assets and her experience with similar companies, the president agreed to extend the asset management project. He offers Mary a full-time position with Medical Multimedia, in charge of capturing, cataloging, and managing the company's multimedia and intellectual assets.

With assistance from the president, Mary defines a KM program in which artists, programmers, marketing, and managers are required to document the process they use in their work, in working with others in the company, and in interacting with customers. Within a year of being hired, Mary has a working KM program in place and functioning. When potential customers call Medical Multimedia for an estimate on cost and delivery time, sales and marketing are able to quickly and accurately predict the internal cost and time required to create the desired product. Additional multimedia that must be created or licensed, the current backlog of work in process, and the additional human resources needed to complete the project on time are all available to marketing and senior managers, thanks to the multimedia database and a library of decision support tools that Mary installed.

Understanding exactly how the 3-D graphic artist performs her work becomes of particular importance when she suddenly leaves to start her own company in the Midwest. Thanks to the process descriptions of her work, Ron is able to hire a replacement with the right mix of skills and bring him up to speed on the program in only three months. Within two years, Medical Multimedia is a profitable, 75-person operation with a record of accomplishment of delivering quality product on time and to specification.

The San Francisco–based Healthcare Productions, which also employs 35 employees, takes a different tack regarding the management of its intellectual capital. Healthcare Productions hires a multimedia consultant to create a multimedia database to track multimedia assets. However, the parallels between the two companies stop here.

The president of Healthcare Productions is resistant to extending the role of the consultant to include intellectual capital. Instead, after six months of work, the multimedia consultant moves on to another company. However, given the competition for artists and programmers in the volatile economy, employees are constantly leaving the company for greener pastures. Even with only three or four employees leaving the company every year, the lag time between finding, hiring, and training a new employee can be up to nine months. As a result, Healthcare Productions can't grow by accepting new clients but is in a holding pattern, simply trying to keep up with the existing demand.

Key Concepts

The story, to be continued in later chapters, illustrates several key concepts regarding knowledge management.

- *Leadership is essential.* Someone in senior management has to own the KM effort. This manager is often termed the chief knowledge officer (CKO) if the task is all-encompassing, or the chief information officer (CIO) or other senior manager may take it on as an additional responsibility. Regardless of who takes the role, it involves achieving buy-in at all levels in the organization. In the story, Mary, who began as a media organization consultant, became the CIO by default, thanks to buy-in from senior management.

- *Knowledge Management works.* The potential benefits of Knowledge Management are numerous and can potentially benefit every type of business, especially those involved in the information technology and service industries. What can a senior manager expect from implementing KM in a corporation? As illustrated in the story of the two companies, under optimum conditions, KM promises reduced costs, improved service, increased efficiencies, and retention of intellectual assets.

- *Knowledge Management requires training.* Employee and manager education is fundamental to the proper operation of every phase of the KM process. As the story illustrates, employees and managers have to be trained to focus on the overall process even while they are attending to specific problems.

- *Expectations must be managed.* Implementing a KM program involves fundamental changes in how employees and managers interact, communicate, command, and get things done. Before reporting lines, responsibilities, and management directives shift to meet the KM demands of the corporation, employees and managers must be prepared for the change. However, since most people fear change, especially if it means disrupting a way of life that they've grown accustomed to, productivity can suffer unless employee expectations are managed proactively. As Mary's role in the story illustrates, an effective approach is to demonstrate the process on a clearly defined, obvious goal that is an easy win—such as cataloging digital image assets. Only after this success was the consultant prepared to convince employees and management of the need to follow general KM practices.

- *Practical Knowledge Management is technology dependent.* Each of the steps in the KM process, as well as tracking knowledge assets, can be enhanced by information technologies. For example, the process of information creation is supported by the ubiquitous word processor running on a PC, and painless acquisition is made possible by the web and associated net-working hardware. Similarly, storing and manipulating huge stores of data are made possible by database servers and software, and getting data in the hands of users benefits from handheld devices and wireless networks that provide anytime, anyplace access to information.

- *Knowledge Management is a process, not a product.* Knowledge Management is a dynamic, constantly evolving process, and not a shrink-wrapped product. Knowledge is an organizational process rather than a static collection of data that can be stored in a database. Typical KM practices in a modern corporation include acquiring knowledge from customers, creating new revenues from existing knowledge, capturing an employee's knowledge for reuse later, and reviewing the predictors of a successful KM initiative.

TIPS & TECHNIQUES

Assessing the Value of Knowledge Management

Before embarking on a Knowledge Management initiative, senior management should have a good idea of its potential value to their organization. In other words, what's wrong with the current model of conducting business? The key questions to ask are:

- How would a KM initiative change the day-to-day operation and management of the organization? For comparative purposes, the operations in companies that make use of KM techniques are described in Chapter 2.

- How would employees react to the overhead of a KM system? Chapter 3 provides a window into the lives of modern knowledge workers and how KM initiatives impact their productivity and relationship to the organization.

- How much could establishing a KM program improve the efficiency and effectiveness of the current business process? Chapter 4 discusses Knowledge Management as it relates to business processes.

- What technologies are available for Knowledge Management, and what are the benefits and limitations? The technological aspect of Knowledge Management is discussed in Chapter 5.

- What are the KM solutions offered by vendors, from consulting to hardware and software tools? Chapter 6 explores the major commercial options available.

(continues)

Reality Check

Although Knowledge Management has a lot to offer, like any other business optimization process, it is by no means a panacea. The major challenges in the KM field are outlined here and discussed in detail in Chapter 8.

Knowledge Management Principles Apply in Varying Degrees

Every successful business operation, from the corner deli to the top Fortune 500 companies, uses Knowledge Management to some degree, even if only in an unsophisticated, ad hoc way. However, the work that some companies engage in is so dependent on individual talent, such as musical or graphical artistry, that the only practical way to capture the relevant knowledge is through a lengthy personal apprenticeship.

Other work can be defined to the point that virtually anyone with a modicum of training can fill a vacancy anywhere in the company. For example, since McDonald's hires workers with a wide range of abilities and experiences, its training program leaves virtually no room for variation in process. Even seemingly insignificant tasks, such as the method in which are fries salted (from the back to the front of the deep fryer rack), are fully defined, leaving little room for misinterpretation of the intended process.

Some work, such as high-end special sound or graphics effects for a movie, is unique to the point that it can be considered magic—it's a special, mysterious, or inexplicable quality, talent, or skill. Tasks involving tacit and, to a lesser degree, implicit knowledge are often considered magic. Salting french fries, in contrast, is a technology based on manufacturing techniques, process optimization, and use of explicit knowledge.

Most tasks fit somewhere in the continuum between magic and technology and within the boundaries set by the characteristics of pure technology and pure magic, as shown in Exhibit 1.6. For example, the tasks associated with salting french fries at McDonald's (represented by the containers of french fries) can all be considered at the extreme technology end of the spectrum. There is a specific process defied for the tasks, and anyone following the process will turn out an acceptable product. At McDonald's, training typically includes having employees watch short training videos—a form of explicit knowledge—distributed by the corporate offices.

In contrast, the ability of a musician to create a one-of-a-kind multimedia experience is considered more toward the magic end of the spectrum, represented in Exhibit 1.6 by the musical notes. The art of making music typically is associated with years of training, and the results may not be replicable by other artists or even by the same artist at a later time.

EXHIBIT 1.6

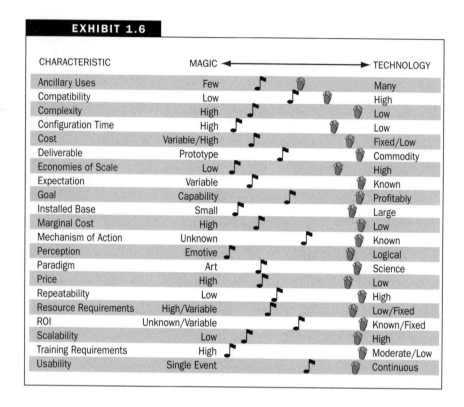

CHARACTERISTIC	MAGIC ←	→ TECHNOLOGY
Ancillary Uses	Few	Many
Compatibility	Low	High
Complexity	High	Low
Configuration Time	High	Low
Cost	Variable/High	Fixed/Low
Deliverable	Prototype	Commodity
Economies of Scale	Low	High
Expectation	Variable	Known
Goal	Capability	Profitably
Installed Base	Small	Large
Marginal Cost	High	Low
Mechanism of Action	Unknown	Known
Perception	Emotive	Logical
Paradigm	Art	Science
Price	High	Low
Repeatability	Low	High
Resource Requirements	High/Variable	Low/Fixed
ROI	Unknown/Variable	Known/Fixed
Scalability	Low	High
Training Requirements	High	Moderate/Low
Usability	Single Event	Continuous

Knowledge Management Isn't Perfect—Yet

In most organizations, Knowledge Management is a work-in-progress, with some subtle and some obvious imperfections. For example, the transfer of data, information, and knowledge from person to person, person to computer system, or one generation of employees to the next is an imperfect process that rarely occurs smoothly and always involves loss of information. Loss of information happens when recording standards shift, when a longer-lasting storage medium requires transfer of information, when data must be migrated between storage locations or translated from one form of representation to another, and when the computer hardware used to interpret the data becomes obsolete.

Significant Legal Issues Exist

Knowledge Management deals with the ownership and manipulation of intellectual property, from copyrighted materials, trademarks, patents, and patent applications to trade secrets. A patent portfolio can add significant value to a company. However, in many instances, intellectual property instruments are useful primarily in defending a court case. What's more, the time lag between applying for patent protection and receiving a patent may be years. Given the time pressure to bring products and services to market, the time and expense of patenting a process or device may make it more feasible for the company simply to keep the information as a trade secret.

However, relying on trade secrets is associated with a risk of employees leaving with proprietary knowledge, even with nondisclosure and non-compete agreements in place. Trade secrets also don't contribute to the valuation of the company to the degree that patents do, since a competing company may file a patent application, potentially barring the company from using its trade secrets. Some companies are attempting to avoid the intellectual property courts altogether by publishing their findings early to prevent the competition from patenting the product or service. This KM approach is especially attractive in the software industry, where virtually any program can be reverse-engineered and replicated in a matter of weeks to months.

Extensive Training and Retraining May Be Required

A significant investment in employee and management training may be required if a KM program is to succeed. Knowledge Management works best when employees and management willingly and regularly contribute to the pool of corporate knowledge. However, willingness without training in process and the use of the technology for storing and retrieving corporate knowledge typically results in costly errors and inefficiency. Most companies with successful KM programs have employee and management training programs in place. For example, a customer service representative who deals with customers via the telephone has to know how to access the list of frequently asked questions (FAQs) on specific topics and how to enter new questions into the system so that the questions and their answers can be made available to others customer service reps.

Overhead Can Be Considerable

Administrative and employee overhead associated with Knowledge Management can cut into efficiency and effectiveness, especially when the typical transaction is very brief. Customers may resent being asked personal questions when they place orders, for example. Saving and submitting customer questions for management to review and include in the store of FAQs in the corporate web site takes time. At issue is whether the expected return on investment in the time spent creating a bank of FAQs or other information makes economic sense.

Knowledge Management Is in Flux

Changes in the KM industry, including abuse of the Knowledge Management vocabulary and concepts by vendors and consultants, obfuscates what would otherwise be simple comparisons of products and services. For example, many database companies and reengineering consultants became KM companies overnight by simply modifying copy in their sales brochures. Companies intent on implementing a KM program have to wade through the unsubstantiated claims from vendors, many of which are made with jargon that serves only to obscure simple (and less expensive) concepts.

Knowledge Management Takes Time

Realistic implementation times for developing a workable KM system range from a few months to years, depending on the complexity of the processes that must be analyzed, the size of the company, the number of employees, and the managers involved. Even in the most technologically challenging KM implementation, the pace of corporate cultural change, not the availability of resources or technology, is the rate-limiting step.

Investment Requirements Can Be Significant

Establishing and maintaining a KM program can be an expensive proposition. A KM system for customer support is an ongoing investment, not a one-time expense. Consider that as soon as the sales reps stop adding questions and answers to the bank of FAQs, the value of the KM system drops precipitously. Eventually, the point will be reached when the time spent searching through the FAQs might not be worth the time or effort of the customer support staff.

Corporate Legacy Must Be Acknowledged

In designing a KM system, it's generally easier to start from scratch. It isn't surprising that the dream of most knowledge officers is to have a new venture built from scorched earth with no history and no legacy data. However, the reality is that most KM programs are implemented in existing companies with established processes for handling orders, deciding on best practices, and dealing with customer support issues. As such, these processes and attitudes will have to be folded into the new KM process. In other words, the KM program should complement the existing business and strengthen existing processes—not turn the company inside out, resulting in processes optimized for Knowledge Management, and no employees to execute them.

Whether Knowledge Management makes sense for a particular business application depends on the business, the corporate culture, and budgetary limitations. The following chapters are designed to help the reader make this determination and to assess the impact of Knowledge Management from the perspectives of cost, effect on quality of service, impact on corporate culture, and how to measure results, and how to best capture and manage knowledge. The book also offers a variety of tactics and strategies that the reader can use to ensure success.

Summary

To compete successfully in today's economy, organizations have to treat the knowledge that contributes to their core competencies just as they would any other strategic, irreplaceable asset. Knowledge Management is fundamentally about managing intellectual assets in a way that provides the company with a competitive advantage. Although Knowledge Management has a lot to offer, implementing a KM program isn't as simple as purchasing a shrink-wrapped package of software. A successful KM implementation requires long-term commitment from senior management; leadership that is attentive to the corporate culture; committed, trained employees and managers; and the appropriate use of information technology.

Where is the knowledge we have lost in information?
Where is the wisdom we have lost in knowledge?

—T.S. Elliot, "The Rock"

CHAPTER 2

Knowledge Organizations

After reading this chapter you will be able to

- Appreciate the application of Knowledge Management in large organizations

- Appreciate the implications of embracing Knowledge Management as an organizational theme

- Understand the responsibilities of knowledge leaders, including the chief knowledge officer (CKO)

- Appreciate how a Knowledge Management initiative is primarily one of corporate culture change

- Recognize the exposure to risk associated with a Knowledge Management initiative

This chapter continues with the exploration of Knowledge Management (KM) that began with the more general issues introduced in Chapter 1 and moves to examine the specific implications of how a KM program affects the day-to-day operation of a knowledge-driven organization. The chapter explores the characteristics of organizations that embrace KM principles from the perspective of corporate management. To illustrate some of these characteristics, let's return to Mary and the Medical Multimedia Corporation.

From What to How

When Mary accepts the full-time position with Medical Multimedia as the person in charge of managing its intellectual assets, she doesn't fully appreciate the magnitude and nature of the task before her. Dealing with the images and sounds produced by the company is straightforward enough. It's clear to virtually everyone why it's important to better manage the company's visible, tangible assets, since they are created, repackaged, and eventually sold at a profit. Thanks to Mary's organizational, process optimization, and communications skills, she is able to understand and then improve on the ad hoc system of multimedia management.

Since everyone in the organization has clear roles regarding their relationship to the production and handling of multimedia assets, no one feels personally threatened by explaining to Mary *what* they do to add value to sound and graphics assets that are incorporated into products sold by the company. For example, before Mary's initiative, each group within the company dealt separately with how to best label and file multimedia assets so that they can be used and located without ambiguity. The programmers are concerned with the physical location of the files and the name of the associated project; artists are concerned with version and creation tool information; while those in the legal department are concerned with license restrictions and expiration dates. Prior to Mary's intervention, each group used its own ad hoc system based on different technology and a unique process. Artists used a database package that ships with their Macintosh computers; the programmers use a proprietary database of their own design on PCs; and the legal group uses a spreadsheet running on a PC; and so on.

When Mary introduces a shrink-wrapped database product and defines a structure that reflects the needs of everyone in the company, there is some resistance to change because it means everyone will have to learn a new system. However, virtually everyone acknowledges the need to integrate multimedia management in the workflow for the common good. In fact, management and many employees are surprised to discover the parallels in needs and practices in the programming, art, marketing, and legal groups. With the help of the in-house technician and support from the chief executive officer (CEO), Mary is able to configure a database application and establish a process that addresses everyone's needs.

Mary's perception of the cohesiveness of the organization changes when she shifts her focus from reengineering the handling of multimedia to managing the intellectual capital of the company. The first thing that she notices is that there is an entrenched, corporate-wide practice of sharing information only within informal, job-specific cliques. For example, the programmers communicate regularly among themselves, tend to go to lunch together, some socialize outside of work, and all keep the discussion of their relative productivity and responsibilities to themselves. Similarly, the artists generally don't interact with employees in other departments unless they are meeting on specific projects that require the coordination of artwork deliverables.

Mary is painfully aware that the cooperation she initially enjoyed from employees regarding *what* they do doesn't extend to the details of exactly *how* they do it, especially from employees with the most specialized knowledge. For example, when Mary interviews the chief graphic artist, Jane, regarding exactly how she archives the images that she and others in her group creates, Jane begrudgingly maps out the process detailed in Exhibit 2.1. In the process that Jane outlines, she takes her images and any associated sounds and indexes them using a controlled vocabulary culled from a textbook—in which all images related to the heart are referred to as "cardiac," for example. She then assigns the indexed multimedia a version number that reflects the generation of the content. The multimedia, now indexed and tagged with

EXHIBIT 2.1

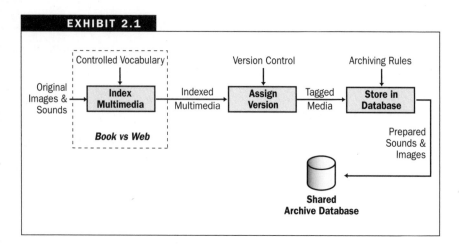

version information, is stored in a database according to rules that define the logical placement of new multimedia in the database management system that is maintained by the in-house computer technician.

When pressed about the details of indexing, Jane initially claims to use a book of standard index terms, with a throughput of about 20 images per hour. However, when Mary asks her to explain why she wasn't using a computer-based lookup tool to provide the controlled vocabulary terms, Jane admits to using a government-sponsored web site to access indexing terms. By Mary's estimates, using the electronic vocabulary tool, Jane should be able to index and archive over 60 images per hour instead of the 20 that she claims. Apparently Jane intentionally hid her use of the web at the index stage of archiving to protect her slack time. Whether because of embarrassment or a perceived threat from the new KM project, Jane gives notice the next day. Within two weeks, Jane is off to the Midwest—outside of the 250-mile radius defined in her noncompete agreement with Medical Multimedia Company—to start her own graphics company.

Jane's departure comes at a critical time for Medical Multimedia. Since the CEO can't afford to lose any more employees, he emphasizes the importance of maintaining existing employees through any KM effort. Together with the head of human resources, Mary and the CEO develop a company policy that recognizes employee contributions with public approbation as well as bonuses and stock options. The policy necessarily reflects the CEO's vision of the company—namely his sense of preserving intellectual capital to maintain an edge over the competition and to increase the value of the company.

Issues

Mary's experiences with Medical Multimedia illustrate several key issues:

- Although Knowledge Management is fundamentally about information and power sharing, the interpretation of Knowledge Management depends on the perspective of senior management.

- The role of the chief knowledge officer or other knowledge manager is situation-specific.

- Knowledge Management isn't process reengineering.

- Senior management must evaluate the potential benefit of a KM program relative to other initiatives.

- The applicability of Knowledge Management is a function of the underlying business model.

- A KM program must respect the knowledge hierarchy by rewarding employees for sharing their knowledge with the organization.

These issues are expanded and explored next.

Matter of Perspective

The corporation was invented in the seventeenth century as a legal entity designed to generate capital while minimizing the risk to the owners and operators. For the first few hundred years, labor was considered a largely undifferentiated raw material used in the capital-generating engine, just like iron, coal, or cotton. Innovation, direction, and vision came from senior management, with the tacit understanding that unquestionably following the corporate vision would be rewarded with a paycheck, a paid vacation, and sometimes even a retirement package.

However, in the years since corporations began, competition, legislation, charismatic corporate leadership, and political realities have changed the nature of the business landscape. In the modern customer-focused service economy, success depends on how management regards employees, especially relating to how a bottom-up approach to innovation is fostered. Innovation in the current economy is about applying new ideas to old problems or applying old ideas to new problems, regardless of whether the ideas are from employees or management. In either case, information is disseminated and applied to improving efficiency and effectiveness, as reflected in the bottom line.

Although this information sharing can occur through an informal encounter of employees with similar interests or those who share a water cooler, proponents of Knowledge Management contend that it won't improve the effectiveness of the corporation unless there is a formal process—and reward—for sharing and documenting ideas and innovations. Without a written tradition, the information sharing becomes nothing more than grumbling about the ineptness of management regarding obvious fixes to the current process.

Creating a culture that fosters sharing instead of hoarding of information and opinions requires much more than simply installing a suggestion box in the company cafeteria. A systematic framework for information sharing, as part of a formal KM program, can provide employees and managers in the organization with clearly defined roles and responsibilities for using knowledge to increase the organization's competitiveness.

The interpretation of precisely how Knowledge Management can support information sharing, archiving, and repurposing depends largely

EXHIBIT 2.2

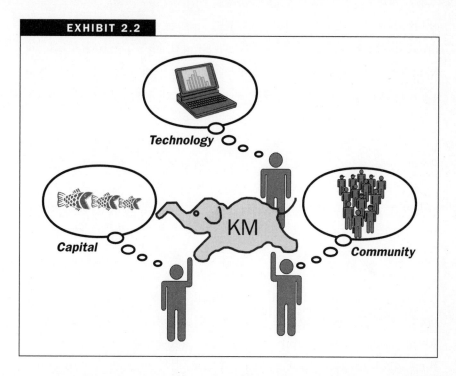

on the perspective of senior management, akin to three blind men appraising an elephant (see Exhibit 2.2). For example, in the case of Medical Multimedia, the CEO is concerned with the competition and retaining intellectual capital, potentially to increase the value of the company for a future acquisition or merger. With this perspective, another motivation for implementing a KM program is to determine the value of the company, based in part on the result of a knowledge audit. Modern service companies are increasingly valued not by their investment in plastic chairs in the cafeteria or PCs on employee's desks but by the intellectual capital of the employees and management. Documenting exactly what intellectual capital exists in the company helps the CEO optimally position his company in the market.

In contrast, senior management with a technical orientation may view Knowledge Management in terms of technology. Typically the chief information officer (CIO) is named as acting CKO or a CKO is hired to work under the CIO. The technical approach to Knowledge Management is especially prevalent in the high-technology arena, where all managers have a working knowledge of, and experience with, technology and what it can do for the company.

A third view is to consider Knowledge Management as a means of strengthening the social fabric of the company. A characteristic of group behavior is that it reflects not so much the needs and desires of the individual members as it does the charisma and beliefs of the leadership as well as the common goals and the structure that defines how individuals within the organization can relate to each another.

One side effect of corporate organization is that it allows the formation of communities of practice, which are groups whose members regularly engage in sharing and learning. These communities contribute to social capital—connections, relationships, and common content—and thereby contribute to the bottom line by increasing innovation, decreasing the learning curve among members, and increasing the dissemination of ideas among members.

Communities of practice, having no agenda, deadline, or accountability, can't be managed. They form because employees are naturally drawn together by similar activities and interests. Although communities of practice can form through informal water cooler interactions, in a large organization with a KM program, they are formally encouraged and supported. That is, in at least one interpretation of a successful knowledge organization, Knowledge Management is much more than simply managing information; it becomes part of the corporate social infrastructure that rewards and supports trust and cooperation among members, including the formation of communities of practice.

Knowledge Management Leadership

Like the definition of Knowledge Management, the types and roles of knowledge leadership in a corporation are usually defined on a case-by-case basis. Although there are dozens of terms ascribed to knowledge leaders by consulting firms, the five main categories of knowledge leadership and their roles in the corporation are:

1. *Chief knowledge officer (CKO).* A strategic, senior management position focused on promoting, communicating, and facilitating KM practices in the corporation. The highly visible CKO typically reports directly to the CEO but may report to the CIO.

2. *Knowledge analyst.* A tactical, lower- to midlevel position that involves learning and personally disseminating the best practices of the organization. Knowledge analysts may use technologies to accumulate and manage knowledge, but the technologies are for their personal use only. The risk of relying on knowledge analysts is that they can walk away with the best practices of the corporation, with no record for those left behind to follow.

3. *Knowledge engineer.* A tactical, lower-level position that is focused on collecting information from experts and representing it in an organized form, typically in computer-based systems, that can be shared and stored in the corporation. Knowledge engineers frequently form the interface between employees and computer technologies, such as expert systems—programs that imitate the decision-making abilities of experts.

4. *Knowledge manager.* A tactical, midlevel position that involves coordinating the work of knowledge engineers and analysts, especially in larger corporations. Knowledge managers may report to the CKO, CIO, or CEO.

5. *Knowledge steward.* A tactical, low-level, and often temporary or informal position normally associated with smaller companies. Compared to the other forms of knowledge leadership, knowledge stewards have the least formal experience with KM principles and usually have other, primary responsibilities in the corporation.

Of the five general forms of leadership, the chief knowledge officer is typically the most visible, least understood, and highest paid member of any KM initiative. Unlike senior managers, a CKO typically has no underlying power base and minimal support staff, and can't make significant decisions without first being empowered by senior management.

Although the typical role of a CKO is in strategically defining a KM infrastructure and in fostering a knowledge culture, as depicted in Exhibit 2.3, the CKO usually wears many hats, ranging from human resources representative and knowledge gatekeeper to process coordinator and public relations liaison. What's more, unless the CKO is politically perceptive and

EXHIBIT 2.3

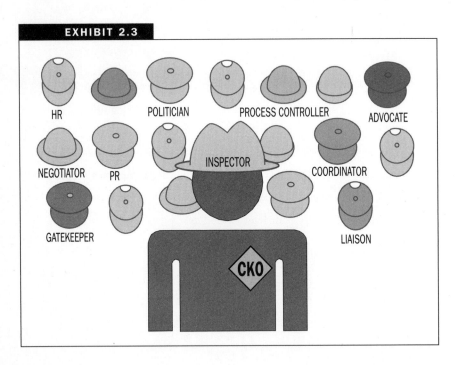

actually facilitates ongoing KM efforts, the employees in the trenches may view the CKO as simply an empty suit that is best avoided.

For the most part, the CKO's responsibilities are distillations of activities already addressed by senior management, but in an unfocused, often informal way. For example, typical CKO responsibilities include:

- *Defining KM policy.* Establishing employee policy regarding the documentation of work processes is one of several tasks that may be championed sporadically by senior management. However, the CKO is in a position to focus on the documentation process in detail and on an ongoing basis.

- *Evangelizing Knowledge Management.* Motivating employees to accept Knowledge Management by illustrating how it will benefit the company and the overall process of asset management.

- *Coordinating education.* A KM initiative involves education, assigning individual responsibility and a point person in each working group who is responsible for assuring compliance with the KM project and for updating information.

- *Safeguarding information.* As an information gatekeeper, the CKO is often in a position to determine access to information and the granularity of information to make available on a need-to-know basis. As described in Chapter 1, most employees and managers need only limited access to the corporate information store.

- *Employee-management liaison.* In many companies, one of the CKO's chief roles is to act as liaison between employees and management. By performing a function that solicits employee input, the CKO can often better encourage employees to go along with the KM project.

- *Technologist.* The CKO must be familiar with the available software and information tools to implement Knowledge Management in an organization. Although the CKO doesn't necessarily need to be from the information technology world, he or she has to understand the tools in sufficient depth to estimate the overhead associated with their use.

One of the most significant issues regarding the CKO position is whether it warrants full- or part-time focus. In most cases, because the tasks of the CKO are simply amplified and focused versions of those performed by general management, there is usually a critical organization size below which a full-time CKO isn't needed. In addition, someone has to be constantly in charge of collecting, organizing, maintaining, archiving and distributing information. Normally, this function isn't performed by the CKO but by knowledge integrators, who are also responsible for actively seeking information to add to the knowledge store.

Because of the variability in what can be expected of the CKO, the requirements for the position are necessarily broad. Although there is no formal CKO certification and no university tracks leading to a degree in

IN THE REAL WORLD

Help Wanted

When the Federal Energy Regulatory Commission (FERC) posted a position job description for its first chief knowledge officer, it listed only two qualifications:

1 Ability to manage knowledge, corporate strategies, and technology for leveraging intellectual capital and know-how to achieve gains in human performance and competitiveness

2 Ability to formulate and implement knowledge management policy initiatives and to direct an organization in the accomplishment of short- and long-term objectives

The chief knowledge officer at FERC oversees the Office of Knowledge Management and Integration. As in many large corporations, the CKO now reports directly to the chief information officer for the FERC.

CKO, most successful CKOs share some general traits. As Mary illustrated in her dealings with managers and employees at Medical Multimedia Company, regardless of the position title, managing a KM initiative requires exceptional interpersonal communications skills, knowledge of best practices in the industry, fluency in information technology, ability to speak the language of employees and management, and management experience.

Knowledge Management versus Process Reengineering

Business consultants and software information system vendors often bundle a KM initiative with other "flavors of the month," from process reengineering and empowerment to various forms of teams. However, although Knowledge Management may be a component of other management initiatives, it's often best addressed as a distinct entity. For example, although many vendors include a KM component in most process reengineering efforts, implementing both simultaneously is at best a waste of time and resources.

A KM initiative typically involves documenting and sharing information about what is, whereas process reengineering is about designing what should be. Knowledge Management is best applied in times of stable processes and as a follow-on to a reengineering effort, not as a parallel process. As illustrated in Exhibit 2.4, this means that KM activities should be avoided during and immediately following process reengineering and major hiring or downsizing activities, whether they are related to the reengineering effort or not. Many KM initiatives fail because Knowledge Management is performed in parallel with a reengineering initiative.

Consider Mary's experience with Medical Multimedia, in which she first deals with process reengineering and then with Knowledge Management. Only after the processes surrounding handling of multi-

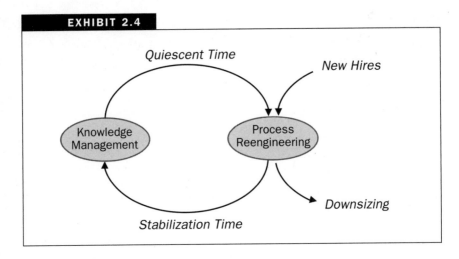

EXHIBIT 2.4

Quiescent Time

New Hires

Knowledge Management

Process Reengineering

Downsizing

Stabilization Time

media were optimized did the KM initiative begin. Since a company in the midst of a reengineering effort is in flux, best practices have yet to be crystallized, and it's a waste of time and resources to document what will likely change in a matter of weeks or months.

As illustrated in Exhibit 2.5, process reengineering is concerned with benchmarking and best practices, implementing alternative business models, and process optimization. The goal is to increase corporate competitiveness by eliminating non–value-added steps, copying the methods of successful companies, and reducing unnecessary employees through intelligent downsizing.

Knowledge Management, in contrast, is about documenting and sharing what is through activities such as:

- *Knowledge audits.* Determining exactly what intellectual capital exists in the company at a given point in time. Knowledge audits can take the form of informal interviews, such as illustrated by Mary's activities in the Medical Multimedia, self-reporting formal paper-based surveys, or through group meetings with management and employees.

- *Collaboration.* Formal task- or project-oriented groups designed to facilitate information sharing. Formal collaboration nor-

EXHIBIT 2.5

Characteristics of Knowledge Management	Characteristics of Process Reengineering
Documenting "What Is"	Defining "What Should Be"
Collaboration	Benchmarking
Communities of practice	Best practices
Knowledge audits	Business model change
Knowledge mapping	Downsizing
Mentoring	Eliminating non–value added steps
Social network analysis	
Storytelling	
Training and development	

mally involves the participation of employees who normally would not work together in the course of their regular work.

- *Communities of practice.* Employees who share tasks, projects, interests, and goals, normally within a specific work area. For example, the programmers and artists in Medical Multimedia formed two communities of practice, defined largely by their common work function. Communities of practice are generally self-forming, dynamic entities.

- *Knowledge mapping.* A process of identifying who knows what, how the information is stored in the organization, where it's stored, and how the stores of information are interrelated.

- *Mentoring.* Experts sharing heuristics, values, and techniques with employees new to processes within the company. Mentoring, like the formation of communities of practice, can be fostered by the corporation but not dictated.

- *Social network analysis.* The process of identifying who interacts with whom and how information is communicated from one individual or group to another.

TIPS & TECHNIQUES

Storytelling: The Larry Chair

Storytelling is a highly efficient form of information sharing because it communicates data, contextual rules, and subtleties of behavior that may be difficult to state explicitly. For example, instead of simply having a rule for the hostess of a restaurant to "seat obese people in the special chairs," employees of the Olive Tree restaurant chain are introduced to proper rules and etiquette through the story of the Larry chair. As the story goes, some time ago Larry, a rather rotund patron of one of the restaurants, complained to management that the chairs, all of which had arms, were too confining. As a result of the complaint, senior management decided that every restaurant in the chain would be equipped with at least two chairs without armrests to accommodate heavier patrons. When girth-challenged patrons enter one of the Olive Tree restaurants, they are discreetly directed to a table with one or more of the special chairs—affectionately referred to as the "Larry chairs."

By relating the story to new employees, management creates a memorable set of expectations. The wait staff understands the purpose of the chairs as well as the need for discretion and the importance of proactively doing whatever it takes to make patrons feel like valued guests.

- *Storytelling.* Otherwise known as the case-based method of teaching, storytelling is a way of communicating corporate values and other implicit forms of knowledge.

- *Training and development.* The traditional method of dispersing explicit knowledge. However, in Knowledge Management, training and development normally involves internal experts from different disciplines, as opposed to professional trainers.

It's important to note that these activities aren't limited to KM initiatives, and rarely are all techniques used in the same initiative and at the same time.

Knowledge Management and Business Models

The viability of a KM program varies as a function of the work performed by the company, how risk is managed, the personality and management philosophy of the CEO, and the underlying business model. Normally, management's philosophy and the business model are in sync, either because a particular form of management is recruited to fit a particular model or because the CEO defined a business model that conformed to his or her vision. For example, CEOs who manage by control or coordination are more likely to devise a centralized business model than are CEOs whose management philosophy is based more on allocating resources or energizing employees.

Exhibit 2.6 lists the applicability of Knowledge Management to common business models.

Some business models lend themselves to Knowledge Management more than others. For example, in Mary's experience with Medical Multimedia, the centralized business model with strong, centralized leadership facilitates the implementation of KM practices in the company. In the centralized business model, there is a high degree of corporate-level control because revenue, reporting, and employee reward are funneled through the corporate management. With a centralized approach, clear lines of communication can result, enabling economies of scale and the ability to standardize the use of knowledge management technologies throughout the organization. Management can send a clear, unambiguous message to employees that investing time and personal resources in the corporate-wide KM effort will be rewarded when it's time for annual reviews and bonuses. However, management doesn't

EXHIBIT 2.6

Business Model	Applicability of Knowledge Management
Centralized	Strongly applicable when centralized leadership rewards employees for KM behaviors
Decentralized	Weak, because a weak central locus of information control makes it difficult to reward sharing of information between disparate groups
Outsourced	Weak, except for knowledge in working with and managing outside vendors
Insourced	Strong for an existing KM program, but weak for a new initiative because of the volatility of employee responsibility and the temporary nature of the work assignments
Cosourced	Variable, depending on the mix of insourced and outsourced activities and the timing of the inception of cosourcing relative to the start of the KM initiative
Shared services	Variable, depending on the maturity of the shared business unit

necessarily have to buy in to the concept of Knowledge Management. If senior management is divided over fully backing a KM initiative, including the sharing of information, then the initiative is likely to fail.

If the Medical Multimedia had been based on a decentralized model in which information is controlled largely by department leadership, Mary would likely have failed at implementing a KM program. In the decentralized business model, there is no central locus of information control, and the local department or company division typically handles reporting and reward for employee performance. The decentralized model provides flexibility at the cost of redundancy throughout the organization and poor integration.

When work is outsourced, there is a loss of control from a process perspective, in exchange for short-term price savings. Business functions are delegated to an outside vendor that serves a number of other clients. Outsourcing usually is done to save costs (including avoiding hiring full-time employees for short-term projects) and done when the job requires a high skill level and is one with a low volume of demand. The downside of outsourcing is the relative lack of control over the vendor's product or services. External vendors can't be expected to reveal their internal processes or trade secrets. However, since the vendor must deliver whatever is specified in its contract, the contracting company has leverage in acquiring certain data.

Insourcing, a strategy in which underused internal resources are redirected, can take advantage of an ongoing KM program but is incompatible with a new KM initiative. Insourcing is used most often as a temporary measure when the workforce must be contracted due to economic constraints.

Insourcing represents a compromise situation, especially from the employee's perspective. Unless the external job market is especially dire or the rewards for handling more work with no more pay are especially rewarding, most employees won't tolerate an insourced situation for long. Because the responsibilities of employees and management in an insourced model are temporary and in flux, a new KM initiative is simply an exercise in frustration.

In cosourcing, which is a combination of insourcing and outsourcing, a third party provides resources as an extension of the company's resources. Cosourcing lies somewhere in the middle between insourcing and outsourcing when it comes to the applicability of a KM program. A company outsources its overflow of strategic processes without giving up control, especially during times of unexpected or seasonal demand. As in insourcing, a KM program is especially helpful in bringing employees and management up to speed in handling tasks that may be new to them, and knowledge of exactly how business processes are carried out can help external vendors more quickly perform the tasks required of them.

Shared services is a business model in which back-end services, such as payroll and accounts receivable, are moved to an external business unit and the parent company remains the main or sole customer. Early on in the life of the shared business unit, revenue reporting and employee reward are likely thought the province of the parent corporation. Later, however, the shared business unit may have no ties to the parent corporation, other than having the parent corporation as a major customer. Because of the flux within the shared business unit, a KM initiative within the shared business unit would be a waste of time. Later, however, when the processes within the shared business unit have stabilized and the unit is a mature company, KM principles can be used to help management and employees of the unit.

Upsetting the Corporate Equilibrium

Ideally, implementing a program designed to improve the bottom line should make life easier for management as well. After all, when it comes to Knowledge Management, what managers wouldn't want to know exactly how the employees they supervise are performing their duties? However, often a KM initiative represents a challenge to all levels of management, especially if managers aren't flexible enough to redefine their roles in the organization.

One challenge is staying focused on managing, as opposed to micromanaging. Management doesn't need to know every detail of how things are accomplished; effective managers intuitively know when to delegate responsibility and operation details to their subordinates. Knowledge of processes to a fine level of granularity leads to the temptation to micromanage processes.

Even though the goal of Knowledge Management isn't reengineering, a KM program is likely to highlight inefficiencies and inequities in the corporation that management may feel compelled to rectify. For example, if a KM initiative reveals that higher-level employees are performing tasks that could be done less expensively by other employees, then the burden of work may shift, pitting the higher- and lower-salaried employees against another. If senior management discovers that it's better for the bottom line of the organization if some of the administrative tasks currently performed by the professional staff are offloaded to administrative staff, the administrative staff may feel cheated and may attempt to sabotage the KM initiative if they do not accept their increased workload.

In addition to upsetting the balance of power in an organization, a KM initiative can threaten both management and employees. From management's perspective, there is the threat of change when and if the CKO leaves. Will the replacement CKO bring yet another set of ideas and technology tools that everyone in the organization will have to take time to learn?

Another issue, illustrated by Mary's experience with Jane and Medical Multimedia, is that employees are usually very protective of slack time. Most employees won't voluntarily reveal all of their timesaving techniques, especially if they've determined through their own know-how to fulfill their job requirements more quickly or accurately. The quintessential tale of slack in industry is detailed by Ben Hamper in his book *Rivethead: Tales from the Assembly Line.* Working on an assembly line in Detroit, he manages to figure out how to work smarter so that he can perform a day's work in an hour or two and take the rest of the day off. As Hamper demonstrates, this guarding of personal slack time isn't necessarily laziness but reflects life in organizations that don't officially reward or even acknowledge knowledge sharing.

Given the likelihood that a KM initiative will at least temporarily upset operations, from management's perspective, there must be a compelling reason for making the corporate-wide investment in an initiative. Often, however, initially there are more questions than answers. For example, how much will implementing a KM initiative cost, both now and over the life of the project? How long will it take to realize the benefits? How much will an initiative detract from the work in progress? What are the risks to the corporation? What of the return on investment, and how can it be measured? As described in more detail in Chapter 7, this latter determination is especially challenging, given that the current rules of accounting say that intangibles are recorded as assets only when they are purchased from another company, not when they are created internally.

The next chapter explores Knowledge Management with a focus on the source of much of the intellectual capital in a knowledge organization, the employee.

Summary

Knowledge Management involves rethinking how management relates to employees. At issue is how to reward the mentors and other knowledgeable employees for the incremental value they create in the company through sharing their knowledge. In many regards, the basic principles of Knowledge Management go against human nature, in that employees, as well as managers, are naturally reluctant to give up their hard-won advantages. This reluctance to share the real core of information isn't limited to business but is also prevalent in academia, which is established around KM principles. Researchers often offer statistical summaries and generalizations instead of raw data, and the technical details of leading-edge technologies are rarely published in a timely manner unless tenure or significant funding is at stake.

True leaders are hardly known to their followers.
Next after them are the leaders the people know and
admire; after them, those they fear; after them, those
they despise.

—Lao-Tzu

CHAPTER 3

Knowledge Workers

After reading this chapter you will be able to

- Understand the significance of the increased overhead on knowledge workers associated with a Knowledge Management project

- Understand the applicability of Business to Employee (B2E) management in a knowledge-management initiative

- Appreciate the concerns of knowledge workers, including decreased job security

- Appreciate methods of developing and maintaining knowledge worker loyalty

- Understand how to encourage the formation of communities of practice

- Understand the importance of education in enhancing knowledge workers' effectiveness and the value they add to the corporation

In the realm of Knowledge Management (KM), employees and managers who contribute significantly to the intellectual capital of the company are called knowledge workers. In practice, the distinction is a matter of degree, in that even manual laborers bring to their company the knowledge of their trade. What's more, whether employees are valued for the knowledge they bring to the corporation depends on whether their knowledge is recorded or otherwise captured for future use.

So-called knowledge organizations—corporations that take a systematic approach to capturing this information—transform employees and managers to knowledge workers, regardless of their actual job titles or duties. But even the best knowledge organizations don't treat every employee as a knowledge worker.

The typical knowledge worker in corporate America works in marketing, intellectual property, engineering, programming, and other occupations that involve more thought than physical labor. For example, artists in the marketing division who produce the media files are typically considered knowledge workers, as media can constitute the intellectual capital of a company, whether the company is a knowledge organization or not. Knowledge workers typically add to the value of the corporation by contributing to the corporate knowledge assets, by documenting problems solving activities, by reporting best practices, and by disseminating information in newsletters, online, and in other publications. In each case, the knowledge worker is either the conduit for or the source of the information.

Customer support representatives are commonly considered knowledge workers because they work with information from customers through direct contact; through interactions through the phone, e-mail, or traditional mail; or through directly observing customer activity in a retail setting. Managers at all levels can be considered knowledge workers if they are involved in creating new revenues from existing knowledge by reformatting and repackaging information in existing markets or introducing existing products into new markets.

Most KM initiatives revolve around knowledge workers, whether they're interacting with customers directly, indirectly through computer systems, or with other knowledge workers and managers. This chapter explores Knowledge Management with a focus on the primary source of intellectual capital, the knowledge worker. To illustrate the challenges associated with managing knowledge workers, let's continue to explore the events at Medical Multimedia.

Unfortunate Loss

Jane started at Medical Multimedia as a part-time freelance graphic artist, working on special projects that the full-time staff didn't have the time or resources to handle. As the company grew, her billable hours increased to the point where it was more economical for the company to offer her a full-time position. Even though she enjoyed the freedom of consulting, the security of the full-time position won her over.

A year later, as Medical Multimedia expanded its product line, the need for an in-house high-end three-dimensional (3-D) artist became apparent to Ron, the manager of the multimedia department. Faced with the prospect of training one of the artists who had been with the company from the start or Jane, Ron decided to ignore seniority and send Jane for training because of her aptitude for the medium. After attending the out-of-state program for six weeks, Jane returned to take full responsibility for all of the 3-D graphics work in the company.

In all, it took Jane about three months to become competent enough to create professional 3-D artwork for the company. Meanwhile, the other artists in the company began to voice their desire to obtain additional company-sponsored education in a variety of graphic arts areas. However, with new time pressures, Ron couldn't afford to send any more artists out for continuing education. Instead, he encouraged in-house education by establishing a weekly pizza lunch during which someone from the group could present some aspect of his or her work and describe the techniques involved. At first, the meeting was little more than a chance to socialize and to enjoy a free lunch. After a few weeks, however, several artists began taking the opportunity to share their knowledge seriously, and the lunch hour became a real opportunity for them to share their experiences and explain techniques and tricks for each of the software packages they used in creating content for the company.

When Mary stepped into her new role of describing exactly how all knowledge workers performed their jobs, the weekly lunchtime education meeting became a forum for discussing the changing landscape of the company, and several members voiced concerns over the security of their positions. With the threat of downsizing on their minds, many of the artists became hesitant to reveal the secrets behind their techniques. Group consensus was that the best approach was to give only as much detail as necessary to comply with the dictates of management, but no more. When it came time for Jane to meet with Mary regarding the details of her work, Jane managed to put the meeting off for almost a month while she explored her career options.

Since she was the only one in the group with knowledge of the $10,000 3-D rendering program, it was progressively easier for her to fulfill the expectations of management, and she gradually became more proficient with the software. Sharing her knowledge of the time-saving tricks that she had learned the hard way would mean giving up not only her proprietary knowledge but also her slack time. With no clear incentive to share her secrets, she avoided Mary for as long as possible—all the while searching the Net for other opportunities.

When she could no longer avoid Mary, Jane agreed to a meeting, during which she revealed one of her techniques. With a follow-up interview scheduled the next day, and no intention of divulging anything more substantial, she gave notice to her manager, Ron. Shortly thereafter, Jane headed west to start a business with a friend, offering high-end 3-D graphics to companies like Medical Multimedia. As a result, the company was set back several months.

The departure motivated management to rethink its position on how knowledge workers are rewarded for contributing to the intellectual assets of the company, including formal recognition of contributions in the company newsletter, and bonuses for exemplary contributions.

Issues

The experiences of the management and the knowledge workers in Medical Multimedia illustrates several key issues:

- Knowledge Management involves maintaining as much of the knowledge worker's relevant knowledge for the corporation as possible.

- A KM initiative must reflect the reality that knowledge workers vary in knowledge, skills, and aptitude.

- In evaluating the contribution of knowledge workers in the modern knowledge organization, there is a significant difference between knowing and doing.

- The knowledge worker–management relationship can't be left to chance but must be managed.

- A KM initiative must include investing in knowledge worker loyalty.

- Continuing knowledge worker education is essential to maintaining the value delivered by knowledge workers.

- Although communities of practice are self-organizing structures, management should facilitate their formation and direction.

- A new business model or management initiative, no matter how innovative and promising, must consider human behavior.

- A KM initiative represents additional overhead, much of which is borne by knowledge workers in their daily work.

Knowledge Worker Relationship Management

Knowledge workers bring certain competencies—combinations of skills, knowledge, and attitudes—to the corporation in exchange for pay, benefits, recognition, a sense of contributing to something greater than themselves, an increased sense of self-worth, the opportunity to work with and learn from others, and, in many knowledge organizations, formal educational opportunities. Within the constraints imposed on hiring and firing practices by unions and the government, companies are free to manage the relationships with their knowledge workers.

For example, in boom times, it's a simple matter to attract and hire the best talent that money and, more important, stock options can buy. In leaner times, when downsizing is necessary, the challenge is developing and growing the best knowledge workers—those who can contribute most to the value of the organization—to maintain competitiveness and to have resources available when the economy rebounds.

Successful companies actively manage their knowledge workers in good times and more challenging times as if those workers were customers. They practice employee relationship management (ERM), a process though which knowledge workers who demonstrably add significant value to the company by contributing more value than the company is investing in them are enticed to stay and contribute their skills and knowledge in exchange for compensation (see Exhibit 3.1). In a knowledge organization, ERM, which applies customer relations management (CRM) techniques to the knowledge worker-company relationship is defined as:

> A dynamic process of managing the relationship between knowledge workers and the corporation such that knowledge workers elect to continue a mutually beneficial exchange of intellectual assets for compensation in a way that provides maximum value to the corporation and they are dissuaded from participating in activities that are unprofitable to the corporation.

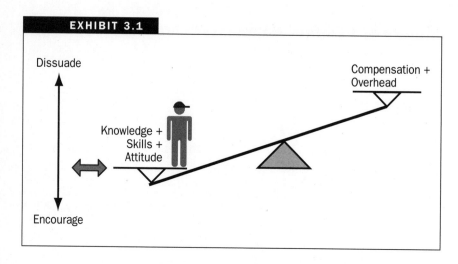

EXHIBIT 3.1

Dissuade

Compensation + Overhead

Knowledge + Skills + Attitude

Encourage

In the context of Knowledge Management, ERM is about managing the relationship between knowledge workers and management, with each contributing to and receiving something from the relationship. Whereas knowledge workers expect compensation for their contributions, corporate management expects demonstrable value and a degree of loyalty. A management that simply follows the wishes of knowledge workers rather than directs them can result in an unwieldy situation in which the "inmates are running the asylum."

In profitable business operations, managing knowledge worker relationships entails saying yes to some knowledge worker demands or requests and no to others, and regularly evaluating the value added by knowledge workers. Companys accrue costs related to ongoing relationships with knowledge workers, regardless of whether those workers add significant value to the company. For example, there is the cost of overhead, which normally includes direct compensation, benefits, social security contributions, physical space, management supervision, human resource services, equipment rental, and education, among others. There is also lost opportunity cost because corporate .esources may be used on one knowledge worker at the expense of a potential hire. A key issue in managing the company–knowledge worker relationship is the consistency of the message communicated to knowledge workers.

Touch Points

Managing the corporate–knowledge worker relationship involves managing the quality and content of communications between knowledge workers and the corporation. From the knowledge worker's perspective, the corporation exists as an array of touch points (see Exhibit 3.2). These points represent opportunities to exchange value—information —whether the knowledge worker is manipulating or creating information, or receiving feedback from management. Knowledge workers interact directly with the corporation at the office through personal contact, via surface mail for some issues, and by e-mail, the web, fax, telephone, cell phones, and wireless devices for others.

Of particular note is that ERM is a dynamic process in a knowledge organization, where what is an acceptable contribution one month may be unacceptable the next. Because of the cost of terminating a

EXHIBIT 3.2

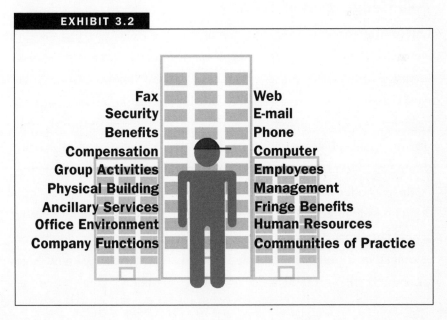

knowledge worker (unless economics dictates it), managing the relationship is focused on shaping his or her behavior. Doing this involves communicating requirements, providing the education and technology tools knowledge workers need to do their job, and facilitating collaboration and leveraging of knowledge internally, within the organization.

The key point is that the message from the corporation to knowledge workers must be consistent across all touch points, especially since every touch point can affect knowledge worker satisfaction. In this regard, every interaction a knowledge worker has with the company through a touch point influences his or perception of the company. For example, knowledge workers expect others in the corporation to recognize their position by name, title, and department regardless of the touch point used. Employees who interact with knowledge workers must be able to access historical data about their interactions with the company, such as dealings with the human resources department regarding benefits.

Knowledge Worker Loyalty

One of the corporation's major intangible assets, and one that can be enhanced through knowledge worker management, is knowledge worker loyalty. Although loyalty is difficult to quantify exactly, knowledge worker behavior that is consistent with loyalty can be quantified. This behavior can be modeled by considering factors that positively and negatively affect behaviors associated with loyalty, such as a worker continuing in a relationship with the corporation even when competing companies offer greater compensation for comparable work.

The issue of knowledge worker loyalty to the corporation typically arises when management is considering whether to invest additional resources in a particular knowledge worker or group of knowledge workers. In the computerized knowledge economy, where someone with knowledge and skills in demand can work from virtually anywhere with a computer and an Internet connection, the issue of loyalty is an important one.

Knowledge worker loyalty can be assessed by modeling loyalty based on the positive and negative contributors to behaviors shown in Exhibit 3.3. Positive contributors to knowledge worker loyalty include difficulty locating alternative employment, the emotional bond between the knowledge worker and the company, the knowledge worker's investment of time in the company, and compensation. For example, the greater the difficulty locating alternative employment, the greater the loyalty effect. Similarly, the more time and energy a knowledge worker invests in a relationship with a company, the more likely the relationship will continue. In addition, the greater the compensation, the more likely a knowledge worker will continue working with the company. The greatest contributor to knowledge worker loyalty, however, is a personal, emotional bond with other people in the company.

The negative contributors to loyalty behavior are numerous employment alternatives and a high level of frustration with the company. The more employment alternatives that are available, the less knowledge workers are likely to stay with the company. Finally, nothing spoils an otherwise ideal relationship faster than a knowledge worker's frustration with management or personal problems with other knowledge workers.

Modeling loyalty behavior shows how knowledge worker behavior can be influenced, depending on which elements in the model are stressed. For example, a generous compensation package and a friendly, supportive work environment contribute to a continued relationship with the company. Conversely, offering knowledge workers little or no increase in compensation at an annual review and ignoring their complaints and suggestions sends a clear message that they should look

EXHIBIT 3.3

Knowledge Worker Loyalty

Contributors to Knowledge Worker Loyalty Behavior:

Difficulty Locating Alternative Employment. The difficulty in identifying alternative employment opportunities that offer comparable compensation.

Emotional Bond. Trust, respect, recognition, camaraderie, and other emotional issues. The stronger the emotional bond, the greater the investment a worker will make in their work, and the more the corporation should value them.

Investment. A knowledge worker's total investment of time and energy, in their relationship with the company.

Compensation. The value the corporation places on the knowledge worker's contributions.

Detractors from Knowledge Worker Loyalty Behavior:

Employment Alternatives. The number of alternative businesses that offer comparable compensation for comparable contributions.

Frustration Level. The knowledge worker's level of frustration surrounding the work environment, especially their relationship with the management and other knowledge workers.

elsewhere for employment. Similarly, inconsistencies in the messages delivered by the company to knowledge workers also send a negative message. For example, encouraging knowledge workers through a generous compensation package and then increasing their frustration level through poor company policies or management can negate the attraction of the financial rewards.

Knowing Versus Doing

Virtually every knowledge worker and manager knows at least two methods of getting things done. Under normal circumstances, there's the official way, which includes going through the formal procedures of discussing, planning, and conceptualizing. Then there's the direct approach, which involves those who actually do the work. These knowledge workers can get something done when it would otherwise be impossible within the constraints imposed by the bureaucracy.

The difference in the two approaches can be described as the process-practice gap (see Exhibit 3.4). Process is routine, managed, official, and based on explicit knowledge. Practice, in contrast, is spontaneous; it sidesteps management and official channels and is based on tacit knowledge and personal connections.

As shown in the exhibit, the role of Knowledge Management is to bridge the process-practice gap. With a KM process in place, best practices quickly become new, standardized processes.

EXHIBIT 3.4

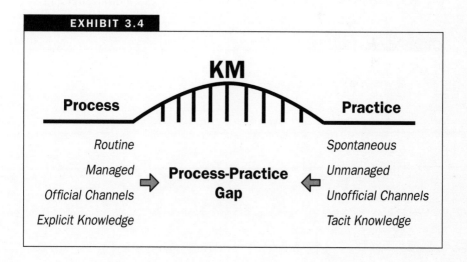

Process	KM	Practice
Routine		Spontaneous
Managed	Process-Practice	Unmanaged
Official Channels	Gap	Unofficial Channels
Explicit Knowledge		Tacit Knowledge

Knowledge Worker Education

In most knowledge organizations, the flow of information isn't limited to contributions from the knowledge worker to the corporation but flows from the corporation to the worker as well. Often this flow of information is through informal osmosis—picking up information and techniques informally through interacting in meetings and working together on projects. Perhaps more important, is the formal transfer of information, in the form of knowledge worker education, which often represents a significant investment of corporate resources. Because of the size of the investment, it's important for management to have a good idea of he likely return on investment (ROI).

One way to estimate likely ROI on Knowledge Worker education is to view each knowledge worker as a value amplifier, converting low- to moderate-value resources into high-value intellectual property, as depicted in Exhibit 3.5. Better knowledge workers offer a higher value multiplier than others; some provide no value gain or even a value loss compared to the invested value. In most case, the value multiplier can be

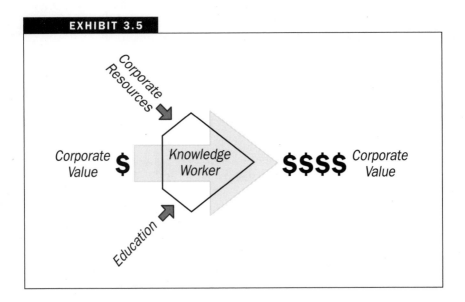

EXHIBIT 3.5

improved through education. However, management has to decide if an investment in education will increase the value multiplier associated with a given knowledge worker sufficiently to warrant that investment.

Part of the challenge in making this determination is that typically there are several unknowns in establishing the ROI of educating knowledge workers. These uncertainties include:

- *Individual differences.* Knowledge workers differ in preferred styles of learning, cognitive abilities, aptitude for certain tasks, drive, and motivation. As a result, some will respond well to the educational experience while others may not benefit.

- *Finite shelf life of knowledge.* In a knowledge organization, procedures and best practices can change in a matter of months, compared to years in a traditional manufacturing company. In a large corporation, by the time a knowledge worker is trained in new skills, a new industry standard could devalue the skill set. For example, in a large news publication organization, reporters originally trained in traditional photographic techniques may need to be educated on digital camera techniques, including how to transfer images over the Internet to corporate headquarters. Reporters who don't receive such education represent a value loss to the company because other news-gathering agencies will respond faster and win assignments.

- *Lost opportunity costs.* The time knowledge workers spend away from work attending seminars and classes, the cost of flights and other transportation, and the cost of on-site instructors and courseware could be invested elsewhere in the company.

- *Knowledge worker turnover.* If knowledge workers are downsized or leave on their own accord, they take intellectual assets with them. The amount of intellectual capital that leaves the company when a knowledge worker departs is inversely proportional to the effectiveness of the knowledge management program.

- *Shifting marketplace.* The competitive advantage conferred to the corporation by knowledge workers with specific knowledge can suddenly diminish because of changes external to the company, such as the release of a new operating system standard or a shift in federal or state laws, or the introduction of a disruptive technology in the marketplace. For example, the knowledge assets of a photo processing chain that deals in developing and printing conventional photographic film is devalued daily as digital photography and digital image processing consume a larger segment of the consumer and professional imaging market. In addition, federal legislation regarding disposal of toxic chemicals used in the production, development, and printing of the traditional film-based photography is accelerating this industry-wide move to filmless photography and a decrease in the value of knowledge of conventional processing techniques.

Fortunately, educational technologies can reduce the cost of education. One of the major advances in knowledge worker education is the use of e-learning (distance learning or computer-based education), which is the use of the web, intranets, wireless computing, and other digital means of educating knowledge workers. This means of dispensing knowledge is expanding rapidly in corporate America primarily because of its lower cost. E-learning combines asynchronous, anytime access with consistent delivery of information to be learned.

As discussed in more detail in Chapter 5, a variety of enabling technologies, including portable digital imaging and sound playback tools, are now affordable and applicable to e-learning. A rapidly growing amount of content also is available. Custom digital courses do not have to be created for generic tasks, given that a wide variety of courses are available online, on CD, and in a variety of digital formats, from e-books and audio on CD and downloaded from the web.

Companies like Charles Schwab successfully use self-managed online education to increase the productivity of its call center workforce and to improve its bottom line. However, regardless of the educational techniques and technologies used, the challenge most companies face is determining the increased value that knowledge workers bring to the company after experiencing the educational process.

Knowledge Worker Recognition

Part of the work in developing a loyal, dedicated workforce is establishing recognition and reward systems to encouraging knowledge worker participation in KM initiatives. Successful managers recognize that knowledge workers are motivated by a variety of factors, of which monetary compensation is only one. Even those primarily motivated by money usually can be encouraged to provide more value to the company by formally recognizing their contribution to the company's bottom line.

One challenge in recognizing the contributions of knowledge workers is that their contributions are often intangible. It may be difficult to quantify relative contributions of intellectual property because metrics are either inappropriate or subject to interpretation. For example, a programmer who contributes 20,000 lines of code to a project may add less value to the company than oner who contributes 2,000 lines of code in one-tenth the time, assuming the code provides the same functionality.

Overhead

Complying with a KM initiative can represent significant overhead in the daily life of knowledge workers. For example, a knowledge worker who is recognized as an expert decision maker may spend a quarter of his time meeting with a knowledge engineer to capture his decision-making process. The knowledge engineer interviews the expert to convert the expert's decision-making process and heuristics into an expert system: rules that can be represented as a series of IF-THEN clauses. Alternatively, the process can be represented as a graphical decision-making diagram to be used with or without a computer (see Exhibit 3.6).

The IF-THEN representation can be used as the basis for a computer program that simulates the decision-making abilities of an expert—a so-called expert system. Eventually the expert system should be able to replicate the expert's decision-making abilities, allowing relatively new hires to use the expert system to make the same quality decisions as the expert. Thus, the ROI for the expert's time is less reliance on the expert and the ability to use relatively naive knowledge workers as expert decision makers. For experts, the reward is a less secure position with corporation, because their decision-making abilities in their area of expertise essentially have been extracted, distilled, and made one of the corporation's permanent assets.

EXHIBIT 3.6

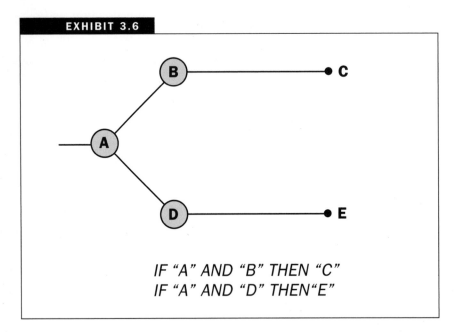

IF "A" AND "B" THEN "C"
IF "A" AND "D" THEN "E"

IN THE REAL WORLD

Exit Strategy

Knowledge Management initiatives are best started at a time of corporate stability, when knowledge workers can be motivated to provide the best-quality information to the system. However, this isn't always possible. For example, Northrop Grumman's foray into Knowledge Management was the direct result of the downturn of the defense industry in the 1990s and the massive layoffs of employees involved in the design and production of the B2 bomber. To capture some of the irreplaceable knowledge that was walking out of the door, the company instituted a KM program in which knowledge engineers worked to capture information about the B2 bomber from employees who had already been given pink slips. Today the company's KM system, known as Yellow Pages, supports over 12,000 knowledge workers through the Internet.

For the nonexpert knowledge worker, a KM initiative often brings the overhead of self-documenting personal interactions with customers, especially with those who call in for support. By having customer support representatives record customer questions and their solutions, a library of frequently asked questions (FAQs) can be built up over months and sometimes years of customer support, allowing new hires (nonexperts) to use the accumulated knowledge to serve customers.

Once the KM initiative reaches steady state, it may be possible to significantly reduce overhead by offloading support to automated programs running on the web. For example, customers may be allowed to access the company's FAQs and their answers from the web, bypassing the telephone interaction with customer support representatives.

Growing Communities of Practice

As introduced in Chapter 2, communities of practice are self-organizing, resistant to supervision and interference. From the knowledge worker's perspective, one of the attractions of communities of practice is that they aren't part of the infrastructure and subject to the rules and formalities of institutional groups. However, since they often form the basis for knowledge sharing in a knowledge organization, it's in management's best interests to somehow support the development or communities of practice without making them a formal component of the corporate infrastructure.

Management can't require knowledge workers to form communities of practice and be enthusiastic. A parallel scenario is seen in organizations that have a newsletter or other publications and user's group associated with membership and require members to join one or more groups. Members may discard the newsgroup's flyers unless they are genuinely interested in the area. The same is true of communities of practice. No one is served by having an employee spend time in a nonproductive meeting.

From a knowledge worker's perspective, a community of practice is often a happenstance meeting of knowledge workers with similar interests and challenges. The composition of the community may shift from week to week, depending on individual schedules, project responsibility, travel, and other chance events. Furthermore, a knowledge worker may belong to one community of practice one month and three the next.

A community of practice is simply a label for old-fashioned networking. A group that plays ball together during the lunch break or after work may constitute a community of practice because it fits in with the scarcest resource of all—discretionary time. Having management dictate groups of common practice based on work factions alone could easily be perceived by knowledge workers as an effort by management to control discretionary time.

Although management can't dictate membership in a community of practice, it can enable its formation (see Exhibit 3.7). Management can offer meeting places where knowledge workers can have lunch and work together. It can organize activities where knowledge workers can network and share ideas and discuss what other departments are doing. It can publish profiles of project descriptions in the company newsletter to alert other knowledge workers of projects that may have synergies. It can send workers to professional conferences.

Often the greatest contribution that a corporation can make to aid in the formation of communities of practice is to support community of practice coordinators. The coordinator is a leadership position defined by the community, not by management, who takes time from his or her regular duties to coordinate meetings, create flyers, send e-mail reminders, and otherwise coordinate the meetings of communities of practice.

EXHIBIT 3.7

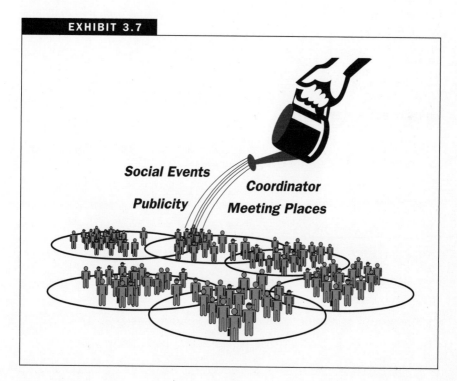

Given the lack of deliverables associated with communities of practice, it's difficult to put a value on any effort to support their formation. For example, how can management put a future value on an idea discussed between two engineers from different departments who met over a game of hoops at lunchtime? Proponents of knowledge organizations believe that communities of practice, as major contributors to the dissemination of information in the organization, often form the backbone of every KM program.

Management as Information Gatekeeper

In the knowledge organization, knowledge workers are the stars of the team, scoring points by contributing to the comapny's intellectual capital. From the knowledge worker's perspective, management's role is like that of a coach: to help establish common goals, to receive work, offer constructive criticism, and supply or orchestrate resources. Like a coach, management also focuses the knowledge worker's attention on the work at hand, in part by handling logistics, resource allocation, and conducting other activities that could distract or even demoralize the knowledge workers.

EXHIBIT 3.8

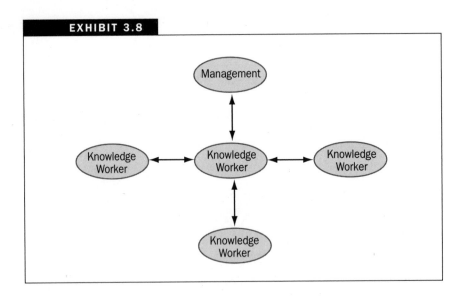

As illustrated in Exhibit 3.8, because management is involved in information and complexity hiding, the knowledge worker's view of the project is necessarily limited to coworkers and direct reporting management.

Because management acts as a knowledge gatekeeper, a knowledge worker may not know, for example, what components of the project are outsourced and which ones are provided in-house, and may have very little idea of senior management's strategy (see Exhibit 3.9).

At issue is how a KM initiative should change the role of managers as information gatekeepers. Although there are exceptions, it's naïve to believe that knowledge workers can manage themselves, especially if they are involved in decisions that have ramifications outside of their areas of direct influence. For example, programmers shouldn't spend an inordinate amount of time telling those in marketing how to do their jobs. However, they should provide marketing with assistance when it's requested.

EXHIBIT 3.9

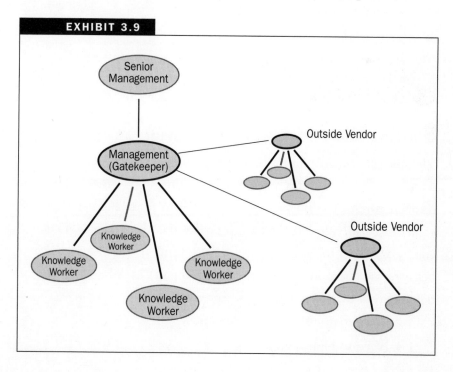

TIPS & TECHNIQUES

Dealing with Gamers

In virtually every knowledge organization, certain knowledge workers will attempt to game the system for personal gain. They'll get involved in the KM process in order to avoid their primary job responsibilities and make themselves known to the knowledge manager or chief knowledge officer (CKO) in order to obtain special privileges and assignments. A problem arises when they have no interest in the success of the KM project, other than as a means of avoiding real work. Knowledge workers who present themselves as shining stars to management but are viewed as slackers by other workers are especially problematic. Knowledge workers who otherwise would have contributed significantly to a KM initiative may not participate, simply to avoid assisting the gamers in their quest for personal gain.

One solution to the gaming problem is to make it clear to all Knowledge workers that they will be consulted on important issues, as opposed to having an open-door policy on all issues. Furthermore, it's important to control expectations, so that a request for a consultation isn't misinterpreted as a request for a decision or even a consensus. The ultimate decision-making responsibility and control should sit squarely with management.

Shaping Knowledge Worker Behavior

The role of management in a knowledge organization often faces competing needs. One need is to set the overall direction of the corporation through control of information. Another is to foster the development of an organization by encouraging contributions from individual knowledge workers. In this regard, it can help to think of a KM initiative as a behavior modification exercise. It should recognize basic human behavior traits, namely that knowledge workers:

- Need to control their environment
- Need to be recognized

- Tend to act in their own best interests unless there is a greater goal
- Tend to follow the group
- Are subject to their own unique behavior traits

Shaping knowledge worker behavior can be encouraged by addressing the need to be recognized and the tendency to follow the group by promoting exemplary behavior through newsletters and the local newspapers. Similarly, many KM initiatives ignore the uniqueness of every knowledge worker and erroneously assume a homogeneous, intelligent, motivated workforce. However, this assumption is valid only to the extent that the human resources department is able to recruit the appropriate knowledge workers through screening and job placement.

In theory, a flat organization that lacks a managing knowledge gatekeeper may offer greater opportunity for knowledge sharing. However, allowing every knowledge worker to share and have access to all available information can be counterproductive, given that everyone desires to control his or her own environment, needs recognition, and tends to address personal interests first. It's impossible for knowledge workers to double as managers when they should be focused on getting their jobs done. Thus leadership, whether in the form of a corporate manager or someone appointed by self-organizing group, is key to the smooth operation of every knowledge organization.

The next chapter continues exploring KM principles and challenges by examining the processes involved in a knowledge organization.

Summary

Knowledge workers are central to the operation of a knowledge organization. Not only do they represent the greatest potential for multiplying the value of a company, but they also represent the greatest risk to value loss. Furthermore, managing knowledge workers is challenging because of the competing goals of encouraging knowledge sharing thorough communities of practice while maintaining control over the general direction of the corporation through information hiding and filtering. For knowledge workers who represent a positive value multiplier, providing consistent supportive feedback through the corporation's touch points, investing in knowledge worker education when economically feasible, and maintaining the processes associated with knowledge worker loyalty all maximize the value that the knowledge worker can bring to the corporation.

Men are disturbed not by things that happen, but by their opinions of the things that happen.

—Epictetus

CHAPTER 4

Process

After reading this chapter you will be able to

- Understand the knowledge management life cycle—its phases and their related issues
- Appreciate the role of standards in the Knowledge Management process
- Appreciate the significance of establishing a Knowledge Management infrastructure

Sharing, archiving and reusing information occurs in most organizations, but leaving these activities to chance decreases the likelihood they will happen. In contrast, implementing a formal Knowledge Management (KM) program, with finite, measurable parameters that can be scrutinized relative to best practices, maximizes the likelihood of success.

In addition, the KM program will have a better chance of adding to the company's bottom line if it is aligned with other key business processes. For example, if customer service representatives are instructed on the importance of documenting each significant interaction as part of a KM initiative yet they are rewarded strictly on the number of problems resolved per shift and not for documenting problems and solutions, the initiative will fail. What's more, they will likely be less effective because of confused communications from management. In contrast, if the KM initiative is orchestrated with a customer relations management (CRM) effort, the synergies between the two efforts can contribute to the success of each other as well as to the company's bottom line.

Part of the task of managing information is understanding the process in which it is created, used, stored, and eventually disposed of and how to accomplish that when the cost of maintaining it is greater than its likely future value. As introduced in Chapter 1, managing information—whether in the form of multimedia for marketing purposes or heuristics for decision making—typically involves eight discrete stages as well as a tracking function. These stages constitute the KM life cycle:

1. Knowledge creation or acquisition
2. Knowledge modification
3. Immediate use
4. Archiving
5. Transfer
6. Translation/repurposing
7. User access
8. Disposal

To begin the journey, consider the unfolding events at Medical Multimedia.

For the Love of Money

Because of a continued downturn in the economy and impending federal legislation placing spending limits on pharmaceutical advertising, owners of the privately held Medical Multimedia conclude that it's in their best interest to sell now, while the company is profitable. Of the prospective buyers, the most promising is the Custom Gene Factory (CGF), a local biotech company. To maximize its position at the negotiation table, the management of Medical Multimedia commissions an independent knowledge audit to establish the value of intangibles in the company—including knowledge worker loyalty and various forms of intellectual property. On the books, Medical Multimedia has a value approaching $15 million, based primarily on tangible assets. However, after the knowledge audit, it's valued at about $30 million—over double the original book value of the company.

With a sale price of $25 million in stock and cash, CGF acquires and absorbs Medical Multimedia into its corporate structure. A $500 million company with about 1,200 employees, including the 75 employees recently acquired in the merger, CGF relies heavily on multimedia to map out genetic structures. It uses these graphics to help sell its services to pharmaceutical firms developing custom drugs for specific diseases and populations.

When the chief executive officer (CEO) of CGF examined the knowledge audit of Medical Multimedia, he was impressed at the value that the KM process added and believed that a company-wide KM program should be instituted. Working with Mary, the chief information officer (CIO), and an outside consultant, the CEO identifies a chief knowledge officer (CKO) who reports directly to the CIO. Mary is repositioned as a knowledge manager for the customer support division of the company, and upper management decides that she will work under the direction of the customer service manager to establish the KM processes, the most appropriate controlled vocabulary, the benchmarks, and the metrics used in the customer support area.

However, after working in that job for one year, Mary realizes that it has become tedious and limited. She's too far removed from the CKO and upper management to effect any real change in the organization, and her day-to-day tasks have become mundane. She gives one month's notice to the manager of her division and announces plans to return to working as a consultant. As was agreed in her non-compete arrangements with

IN THE REAL WORLD

Recycled Employees

During lean periods, middle managers are usually among the first employees to go. While this is a quick method of reducing payroll expenses, it also results in the loss of significant knowledge about how to get things done in the company. To reduce the loss of knowledge resources during a downsizing operation, Caterpillar recycles some of its middle managers into trainers at its Caterpillar Training Institute in western Australia, which offers courses on topics from forklift safety operation to off-highway truck systems.

Medical Multimedia and CGF, she is free to consult for any companies as long as she doesn't disclose proprietary information.

Senior management's first concern is that Mary will leave the company with a great deal of knowledge that can't be replaced. Furthermore, her knowledge about the company's KM processes would be invaluable in the hands of a competitor—even if it were not explicitly re-created. As a consultant to a competitor, Mary could reapply her KM skills, much of which she developed while she worked with Medical Multimedia.

Short of resorting to legal action and creating an adversary, the best that CGF can do is offer Mary a bonus to work with a knowledge manager from another division to capture some of the heuristics that she developed while working with Medical Multimedia. Mary declines the offer of a bonus and takes the vacation time that is due her. She reappears two weeks later, offering her services directly to the CKO, one day per week, and at a considerably higher rate that she had been paid as an employee. The CKO readily accepts, and Mary begins work on the much more interesting and company-wide aspects of Knowledge Management in the biotech company.

Issues

Custom Gene Factory's acquisition of Medical Multimedia and the associated activities illustrate several key issues associated with a KM initiative:

- Knowledge workers involved directly in the KM process may be the company's most valuable assets.

- If it is to be successful, Knowledge Management is a business process that has to be managed like every other major business initiative.

- It is virtually impossible to prevent the repurposing of tacit knowledge by workers who leave the company. For example, in the story, management can't stop Mary from leaving the company and using her tacit knowledge in the service of the competition.

- Knowledge audits are commonly used to quantify the value of a company's intellectual assets. A series of knowledge audits can demonstrate the effectiveness of a KM initiative.

Life-Cycle Overview

The duration of the Knowledge Management life cycle is a function of the availability of the technologies that enable each phase and of the nature of the information, the difficulty of archiving the information, and other external factors. For example, some business information, such as tax information, must be retained or archived indefinitely to comply with federal, state, or local law. Other information may be critical to maintaining the value of the corporation, such as knowledge of core processes in the company.

As illustrated in Exhibit 4.1, each phase of the KM life cycle is associated with issues, input data, support mechanisms, and output data. The difference between the input and output data depends on the processes

EXHIBIT 4.1

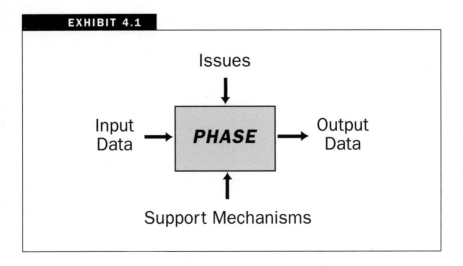

involved in the particular phase of the KM life cycle. For example, in the archiving process, the output data are indexed according to a standard or controlled vocabulary, whereas in the translation phase, the format of the information is converted to a more useful form.

Issues

The issues relevant to each phase in the Knowledge Management life cycle depend on the phase as well as the type of knowledge involved. For example, for highly sensitive medical, legal, or financial information, security is a key issue. In contrast, for information that will be published on the web for general consumption, verifying ownership and copyright may be primary concerns. The primary issues in the KM life cycle, each of which is relevant to different degrees at each phase of the life cycle, include:

- Economics
- Accessibility
- Intellectual property
- Information

- Infrastructure
- Management

Economics

Every phase of the KM life cycle has an associated resource requirement in terms of money, time, technology, overhead, and physical space. Costs typically are expressed in cost per quantity of information accessed, manipulated, or stored. In this regard, the value of the data or information handled by the KM system reflects both the cost of replacement and resources already invested in acquiring the information. The economics of the KM life cycle also should provide for unplanned events. For example, a KM initiative must have enough economic reserve to survive data loss due to unavoidable accidents, ranging from human error to hardware failures and software incompatibilities.

Accessibility

The accessibility of information in a KM system is a primary concern of knowledge employees and managers. Accessibility issues include access privileges—who within the organization has access to specific information and the type of access allowed. Access privileges typically are stratified on a need-to-know basis and by level in the organization. For example, whereas the CEO may have access to information throughout the organization, a knowledge worker in, say, customer support may not have access to information in the human resources department. The type of access to information commonly varies as a function of the knowledge worker's role in the organization. The librarian may be able to read, modify, and even delete information from the KM system. However, a front-line knowledge worker, such as a customer support representative, may be able to read and write information but not modify or delete information already in the system.

User authentication and security are directly related to access privileges. Authentication includes the methods used to verify that the users are who they say they are. In automated KM systems, authentication based on username and passwords is increasingly supplemented with biometric systems that rely on images of the user's fingerprints or retina. Security involves keeping unauthorized users from accessing, modifying, or destroying valuable information. A related issue is privacy, which is accomplished by maintaining certain information out of the reach of those without access privileges and need to know. In most KM programs, the ability of someone in the organization to modify information once it has been created or added to the system is especially guarded and tracked.

Access time is also a function of the ability to locate specific information in any phase of the KM life cycle, which is directly related to the methodology and vocabulary used to archive, locate, and retrieve information. As detailed in Chapter 5, the methodology and technology used to track the location and version of information in the KM life cycle also affect accessibility.

Intellectual Property

The intellectual property issues associated with each phase of the KM life cycle have legal and practical implications. For example, there is the issue of specific intellectual property rights, such as moral rights, that may allow a knowledge worker to claim authorship of information even if other intellectual property rights have been assigned to the company. There is also the issue of the amount of author involvement in the KM life cycle once the information has been created. With information acquired outside of the corporation, such as stock artwork or work for hire, the issue of ownership verification, the process of verifying intellectual property ownership, arises.

Information

In automated KM systems, information is commonly in the form of electronic files. In manual KM systems, information may be in the form of a book, card file, or file folder. These formats afford different kinds of intellectual and social activity.

Then there is the issue of finding a standard nomenclature familiar to all knowledge workers who need the information, despite their different backgrounds. The language can range from graphical representations of decisions, numerical relationships, and textual descriptions in English or other language, to IF-THEN clauses that can be read by machine. A related issue is file naming, the labeling of information prior to or instead of indexing it with a controlled vocabulary; naming may be ad hoc or systematized, as determined by the author or management.

Reversibility, the ability to reverse or negate changes to the information that occur during the KM life cycle, is a chief concern of those wishing to repurpose information. Some changes, such as disposal, are irreversible, because information may be lost in the original translation process, whereas other changes are fully or partially reversible. For example, original data normally can't be reconstructed from summary statistics. Versioning, the ability to track incremental changes to information, such as modifications, is key to allowing reversibility. Translating information from one form to another is usually fully reversible.

Infrastructure

A functional, supportive infrastructure enables the application of information technology to one or more phases of the KM life cycle. Core infrastructure issues include the nature of the supporting computer and communications hardware; the frequency, cost, and regularity of hardware updates; and the information storage capacity of a manual filing facility or computer system. In both physical and computer-based KM systems, local storage capacity affects speed of access and has security implications. For example, storing all information in a local database makes the entire KM system more vulnerable to accidental loss due to hardware failure, fire, or flood.

There are also software issues, such as the performance and version of the computer's operating system and network; the functionality, ease of use, performance, and cost of other software tools used in an automated KM system; and the availability of software updates, an area especially relevant in long-term archiving and maintenance of information.

Management

Management has a role throughout the KM life cycle. The key managerial issues are quality control, including the degree to which quality control standards are established and followed, and process stability, which includes the stability of each phase of the KM life cycle as well as that of the overall life cycle. Management exerts control first by naming a librarian, who is in charge of the overall KM process and of the day-to-day upkeep of information in the system. Management also exerts control through sign-off or formal acceptance of the work involved in each phase of the KM life cycle.

Support Mechanisms

Just as the key issues apply variably to each phase of the KM life cycle, the support mechanisms are more relevant to some phases than others. The primary support mechanisms or methods in the life cycle include technology, standards, knowledge workers, and management.

Technology

The technologies involved in the KM life cycle, described in depth in Chapter 5, include communications and collaborative systems, such as the

Internet and other networks; a variety of tools to manipulate, transform, and create information; and database technologies that can enable the rapid storage and retrieval of information.

In addition to general technologies, specific tools enhance and secure the flow of information in the KM life cycle. For example, security systems provide data encryption and user authentication; software systems and processes insure the version of information used is appropriate to the intended use; and program instrumentation is an automated means of tracking use of information throughout the KM life cycle. Other niche technologies range from erasure programs, the equivalent of paper shredders in an office environment, to decision support tools to help a librarian or management decide, for example, what information to archive and what information to destroy. Expert system technologies can help guide knowledge workers and other employees by providing them with access to instant expertise. Even the media used to store information has implications regarding ease of use, transport, and long-term storage.

Standards

Standards provide the basis for control and consistency of information. In the context of supporting a KM initiative, standards are extensions of the KM process because they encapsulate rules and heuristics and thereby represent knowledge. Standards also represent best practices, the best way of accomplishing Knowledge Management. Furthermore, standards provide benchmarks for comparing performance. As such, they provide a basis for optimizing KM phases.

Knowledge Workers

As Mary's career illustrates in the story of Custom Gene Factory, knowledge workers are some of the most important assets in a knowledge organization. In supporting the KM process, knowledge workers contribute through activities ranging from self-reporting and documenting company processes, to knowledge engineering, which involves a formal means of extracting knowledge from an expert and converting this information into heuristics and flow diagrams.

Management

In most knowledge organizations, management's role is to provide support and direction for knowledge workers. In this role, management directly influences the KM life cycle by aligning and integrating its phases with the overall business strategy and other business initiatives. Management is also responsible for providing an environment supportive of KM activities, from an efficient work environment to safe storage areas for magnetic media and printed documents. By helping define corporate policy, management can help support each phase of the KM life cycle.

Management also defines and then assigns access and use privileges to the information in the KM system, through the authority and responsibilities of a librarian. The librarian, as a manager or upper-level knowledge worker, is typically at least partially responsible for every phase of the KM life cycle. For example, the librarian normally is charged with creating and managing a formalized means of capturing user feedback to determine what information is used, what isn't, and who in the organization is using it. Armed with this information, the librarian works with the CKO, knowledge managers, and knowledge workers to determine what information to archive, what to dispose of, and what to allow to become unusable though benign neglect.

Each of these issues and support mechanisms is discussed more fully below.

Creation and Aquisition

In the creation an acquisition phase of the Knowledge Management life cycle, information is authored internally by knowledge workers, acquired through outsourcing, or purchased from an outside source. As illustrated in Exhibit 4.2, this phase starts with a requirements specification that provides the author or acquiring agent with a description of the information needed. The information can take the form of questions presented to customer service representatives; decision-making heuristics used by expert knowledge workers; and designs, illustrations, and schematics of devices and services sold by the company. It also can be process descriptions and personal best practices. External sources of information are increasingly significant in most knowledge organizations, especially given

EXHIBIT 4.2

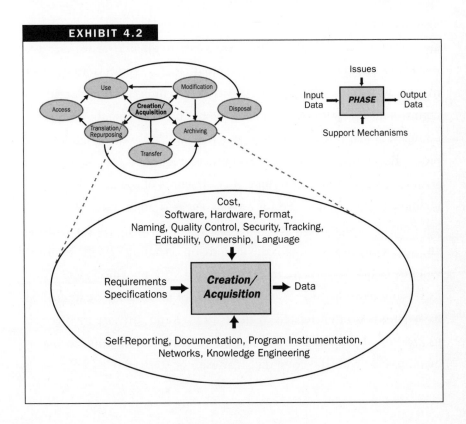

the affordability and ready availability of commercial databases on every topic from current publications to industry-specific processes in fields like engineering, law, and medicine, and genomics.

In Exhibit 4.2, the primary issues associated with the creation and acquisition of information in the KM life cycle include cost, the enabling hardware and software technologies, the format and naming of information, quality control, security, and the means of tracking of information. In addition, the editability of the information, ownership, and even the language used to represent the information are significant.

Information is never free, even if the direct costs of creating and acquiring information can be avoided. Over time, the indirect costs, including tracking and archiving, can easily exceed direct costs. Indirect costs commonly include the hardware and software infrastructure. For example, in automated KM systems, computer hardware and software are enabling technologies. However, issues frequently arise over the make and compatibility of hardware used to create and capture information. In many companies, the artists and architects favor Macintosh-compatible hardware, whereas engineers and accountants favor PC-compatible hardware. Similarly, when mobility and portability are required, hand-held and laptop computers frequently are employed. As with desktop systems, often there are differences of opinion over which technologies are best suited for a particular KM application.

Software issues range from the best applications to use for creating and acquiring information to the underlying operating system. Similarly, when network systems are involved, the network operating system and its versions also can be an issue. The format of information in automated KM systems is often related to the hardware and software involved in its creation or acquisition. Issues arise when the information format is incompatible with the computer hardware or software.

In addition to infrastructure issues, there are process-oriented issues, such as the naming system used by the information author or acquirer. If the information will be used immediately and not archived, the naming system used by the author has little relevance. However, if the information is likely to be repurposed, a controlled vocabulary or at least an agreed-on system should be used to label the information. For example, white

TIPS & TECHNIQUES

Validating Best Practices

Collecting and disseminating best practices may be difficult, but validating their contribution to the bottom line is even more challenging. Even with a database, an intuitive, easy-to-learn front end, multiple points of access, and a streamlined process for capturing best practices, the system may lay dormant unless the quality of data stored in it can be validated. That is, simply because a knowledge worker submits what he or she thinks is a best practice doesn't mean it should be disseminated throughout the organization. This situation exists on the Internet, where anyone can start a web site and self-publish information on any subject, even though he or she may have no expertise in what is being presented. What one knowledge worker considers a pearl of wisdom may be viewed as ludicrous or simply wrong by another.

The solution used most often in industry parallels that used in academia, where articles submitted for publication in a print or online journal are first peer-reviewed by experts in the area. In many cases, the original article is either rejected outright or accepted provisionally with editorial and content changes. Similarly, ideas submitted from employees go through a screening process. However, instead of outright rejections which might simply state that the topic has been covered or that it's being covered by some other method, to encourage future submissions, employees can be sent a gracious letter or e-mail thanking them for their submission.

papers produced by a company's engineering department may use a sequential name, such as "ENG ###", where "ENG" stands for engineering and "###" is a placeholder for the next number in the sequence of white papers from the department.

The tools used to create information affect its editability, which can be an issue if translation and repurposing are likely in the future. For example, a text document can be authored in Microsoft Word, allowing the document to be easily edited by someone with access to it. However, although other knowledge workers may easily access a document created in Adobe PDF, the document can't be modified because editors are generally not available for the proprietary PDF format.

Finally, information ownership and other intellectual property issues often are established during creation or through acquisition. For example, information may be licensed from outside the organization for a particular purpose or project. As Mary illustrates in the story, ownership of tacit information is difficult to quantify.

Modification

In the modification phase of Knowledge Management, the information is modified to suit the immediate and likely future needs of knowledge workers and management. The primary issues related to the modification phase of the KM life cycle, illustrated in Exhibit 4.3, include moral rights, the degree of author involvement, assigning responsibility for the sign-off process, making decisions as to the reversibility of modifications to information, and verifying ownership of information.

Ideally, modifications to information should be reversible. However, full reversibility may require significant storage space and thus be impractical. For example, images may be stored as original, uncompressed TIFF documents or saved as space-saving JPEG documents. Using a JPEG compression scheme may provide a 10- to 100-fold

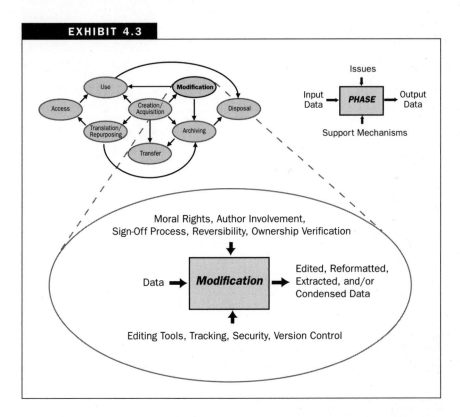

EXHIBIT 4.3

decrease in file size compared to the original, but the compression process isn't fully reversible because the transformation from a TIFF image to a JPEG one involves data loss. The greater the compression, the greater the information loss. Finally, someone in the organization has to have the authority to sign off on the modification, indicating that it, like the original information, is correct.

As illustrated in Exhibit 4.3, the key support mechanisms for this phase of the KM life cycle include editing tools, tracking information, security, and version control. Generally information is modified with the aid of tools, such as graphic programs and text editors. Version control, using software tools to track of versions of documents and other information, is key to locating the intermediate products of internally authored information.

Use

In this phase of the Knowledge Management life cycle, the information is employed for some useful purpose. The range of potential uses for information is virtually unlimited, and depends on the industry and the needs and activities of knowledge workers within the organization. For example, the information may be incorporated into applications for sale or licensed to third parties.

The key issues in the use phase depicted in Exhibit 4.4, include usability, accessibility, security, intellectual property, and tracking. For example, not only must the information be easy to use in the form provided, but it must be easily accessed by those with the appropriate privileges. In addition, use of specific information may be restricted by licensing, moral rights, and other intellectual property controls.

EXHIBIT 4.4

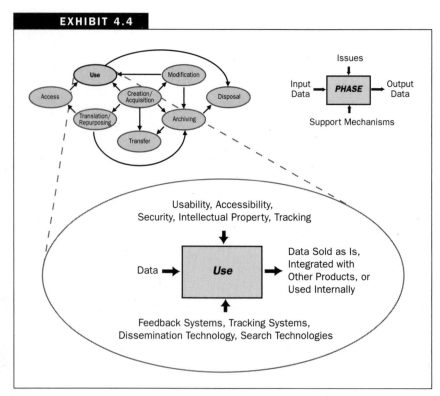

Key support mechanisms in the use phase of the KM life cycle include feedback and tracking systems as well as a variety of dissemination and search technologies. Feedback from automated tracking or direct user feedback is key to improving the processes involved in the KM life cycle. In addition, technology-enabled information dissemination systems, from expert systems and decision support tools, to visualization systems, increase the value of information for specific uses. Similarly, search engines and other technologies allow knowledge workers to navigate through vast collections of information efficiently and effectively.

Archiving

Archiving information involves storing it in a form and format that will survive the elements and time and still be accessible and usable by knowledge workers in the organization. Archiving can involve printing, making electronic copies in several formats on a variety of media, or even outsourcing to an off-site storage facility accessed over the Internet.

Some of the key issues related to the archiving phase of the KM life cycle, depicted in Exhibit 4.5, include access time, provision for security and privacy, selection versioning and indexing of information, the location of archives, the cost of archiving, and the various technologies used, especially those used to filter or select information. From the user's perspective, access time—the time to retrieve specific information from the archive—usually is the most significant day-to-day issue. Depending on the technology underlying the archiving process, access time can range from a few seconds to days, with the greatest delays associated with printed information.

Archives, especially central repositories, are attractive to hackers because of the concentration of information in one place. Making multiple archives protects against fire, flood, or other natural disasters but presents a greater security risk because multiple sites must be covered

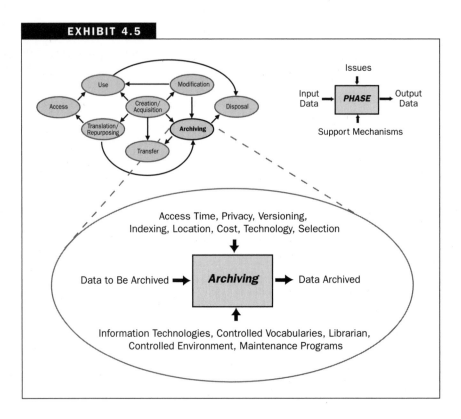

EXHIBIT 4.5

with the same vigilance. Similarly, maintaining the privacy of information in an archive can be challenging because of the potential intervention of hackers or internal knowledge workers.

Besides providing ready access to information, archiving involves a filtering process that is a function of the quality and importance of information, cost of archiving, and the likely need for the information in the future. For example, in archiving phone support logs for the creation of a frequently asked question (FAQ) online database for internal customer service representatives, relevant questions and answers may be flagged for editing and archiving for use in the future. Because the information may go out of date with changes in the product line, there must be some efficient, automated means of identifying all FAQs related to a discontinued product.

The most important support mechanisms at the archiving phase of the KM life cycle include a variety of information technologies, from database management systems and controlled vocabularies to expert systems. The longevity of the information in the archive is a function of having a controlled environment, maintenance programs in place, and a librarian to oversee the archiving process. Archiving lends itself to a secure, controlled storage environment that is safe from natural and artificial threats, from fire and flooding to hackers. Similarly, since file formats, operating systems, computer hardware, and even media have a finite life span, maintenance programs that specify periodic conversion to new operating systems and most popular file formats will ensure that the information is accessible in the future.

Transfer

The transfer or communications of information from one person or place to another is a prerequisite for an efficient Knowledge Management system. As illustrated in Exhibit 4.6, the key issues in the transfer phase of the KM life cycle include cost, security, and transfer time. The cost per quantity of information communicated from one point to another may be significant, especially if there isn't an existing networked infrastructure. In addition, the security of information is always an issue, and it is especially critical when the information is being transferred across a public network, such as the Internet or a wireless or telephone network. Transfer time—the time it takes to move information from one point to another in the organization—often defines the usability of a KM system. In most cases, the shorter the transfer time, the more usable the information.

The primary support mechanisms in the transfer phase of the KM life cycle include networks and, in some instances, physical transfer. Corporate intranets, the Internet, and the web are all enabling technologies

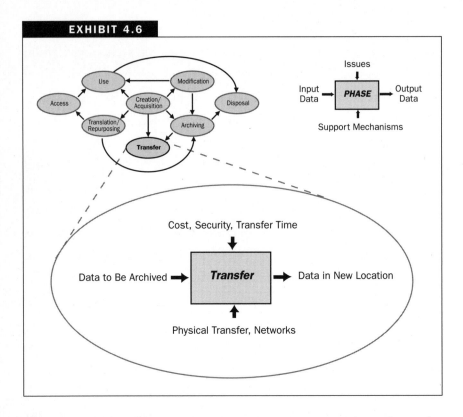

EXHIBIT 4.6

that support virtually instantaneous communications throughout the KM life cycle and shorten the transfer time. However, for some applications, including ultrasecure electronic digital information as well as digital media-based communications, physically delivering media from one point to the next is the way to transfer information.

Translation/Repurposing

In the translation/repurposing phase of the Knowledge Management life cycle, information is translated from its original form into a form more suitable for a new purpose. For example, a table of numerical data may be transformed into a three-dimensional graphic, a sound file might be translated into a graphic or sonogram, or the data in the table might be condensed into a concise statistical summary.

Exhibit 4.7 illustrates the key issues at this phase of the KM life cycle, which include reversibility of the translation process, the moral rights of the author, ownership verification, and author involvement in the translation and repurposing process. Translation and repurposing may be constrained by the intellectual property rights of the original author or licensing agency. For example, the original author may have retained the moral rights to the information. Often this constraint can be avoided by involving the original author in the translation process.

When a complex translation or significant repurposing of information is under way, author involvement often can ensure that the context and accuracy of the information are maintained. Because the translated information may not resemble the original information, many times

EXHIBIT 4.7

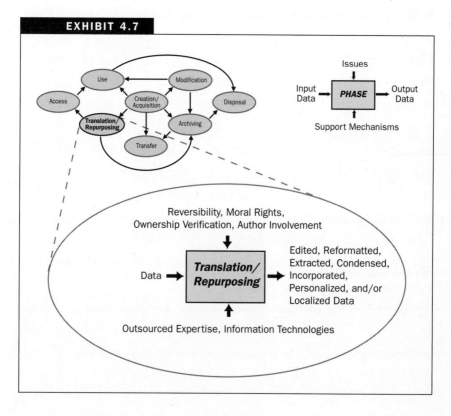

verifying ownership of the information is critical, especially if the information is to be repackaged and sold.

The most significant support mechanisms in the translation/repurposing phase of the KM life cycle include outsourced expertise and a variety of information technologies. External vendors usually are happy to provide translation services to companies that don't have the time or the resources to perform the translation in-house. For some applications, software programs, specialized translation hardware, and other technologic solutions are available to support automatic translation.

Access

A characteristic of most Knowledge Management systems is information hiding, in that all information in the corporation isn't openly available to everyone. Typically, limited access to the information is provided to knowledge workers as a function of their position in the company and their need to know.

Access to information also can be limited by the sheer volume of information available. For example, in a KM system with hundreds of thousands of FAQs available to customer support reps, accessing the particular FAQ and response for the problem at hand can present a significant challenge. A parallel situation exits on the web, where the challenge is culling the desired information from the vast stores of information available. All too often, searching for a term or key word brings up a list of tens of thousands of possible web sites that may have little or no relevance to the desired information.

In Exhibit 4.8, the most significant issues related to the access phase of the KM life cycle are and information security, and cost, selecting the most appropriate technologies, and knowledge worker authentication. The cost of accessing information can vary considerably, depending on

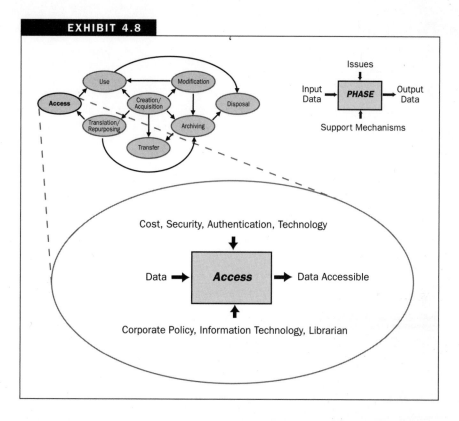

EXHIBIT 4.8

corporate policy, the interaction required from the librarian or other support staff, and the cost of the underlying technology infrastructure.

In addition to search engines, biometric user authentication systems, graphical user interfaces, and other information technologies, key support mechanisms in the access phase of the KM life cycle are corporate policy and the librarian function. Access to corporate information is fundamentally defined by corporate policy, which specifies, for example, who needs access to specific information. In addition, the librarian function, performed by a knowledge worker, manager, or computer program, is necessary to control expectations, prevent misuse of the underlying technology, and ensure that corporate policy is enforced.

Disposal

The ultimate destiny of information, whether from the scourges of time, short-term benign neglect, or intentional disposal, is destruction. Although all information collected and generated in the course of conducting business may be valuable to someone at some point in the future, from a practical perspective, information with limited future value is discarded to save space and reduce overhead.

The method of identifying what information to save and what to destroy should follow corporate policy as well as governmental rules regarding business records. As illustrated in Exhibit 4.9, the primary issues surround the destruction of information in the disposal phase of the Knowledge Management life cycle are cost, the most appropriate

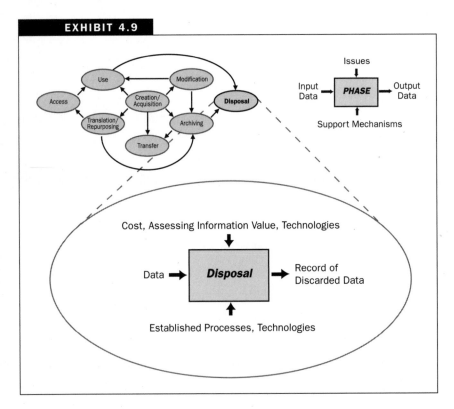

EXHIBIT 4.9

level of security, assessing the value of information, and a variety of enabling technologies.

Throwing away information isn't free, especially if the information must be processed extensively before disposal. For example, the level of security needed at this stage of the KM life cycle can be extremely high, depending on the nature of the information to be discarded. Since this may be the first and only time that information generated within the organization is handled by the public disposal system, the potential for corporate espionage or even accidental discovery exists. For example, simply throwing old servers and PCs in a Dumpster may allow the competition to recover the hardware and explore information on the hard drives. Someone, such as the librarian, must have the authority to assess the value of maintaining information in the corporation versus disposing of it.

Knowledge Management Infrastructure

The discussion of the Knowledge Management life cycle has assumed that an infrastructure of sorts provides the support necessary for each phase of the life cycle. This infrastructure consists of tracking, standards, and methods of insuring security and privacy of information. In most organizations, this infrastructure brings with it considerable overhead for both the company and the knowledge workers. For example, generating and maintaining information is difficult enough, but it also must be tracked, just as a book is tracked by a librarian in a public library.

Besides merely tracking information at every phase of the KM life cycle, standards for processing and handling information must be followed to guarantee security, accuracy, privacy, and appropriate access. Just as libraries don't condone readers replacing books on the shelves for fear that the books might be shelved incorrectly and therefore be temporarily "lost" to other patrons, knowledge workers must abide by rules established to maximize the usefulness of information throughout the KM life cycle.

Chapter 5 continues the discussion of the phases of the KM life cycle, from the perspective of the vast array of technologies that can be applied to enable the infrastructure and the individual phases of the life cycle.

Summary

The Knowledge Management life cycle is perhaps best described as a web of interrelated phases. Each phase is associated with issues that must addressed by supporting mechanisms and can be enabled by information technology. Most of these issues revolve around economics, accessibility, intellectual property, the underlying infrastructure, and the commitment and active role of management in setting policy. In addition, the issues regarding the information itself need supporting mechanisms, such as establishing and enforcing standards, utilizing the contribution of knowledge workers, and managing the overall process.

> *Do not be desirous of having things done quickly. Do not look at small advantages. Desiring to have things done quickly prevents their being done thoroughly. Looking at small advantages prevents great affairs from being accomplished.*
>
> **—Confucius**

Technology

After reading this chapter you will be able to

- Appreciate the range of available technologies that can support a Knowledge Management initiative

- Understand the significance of selecting or developing a controlled vocabulary as part of a Knowledge Management initiative

- Understand what differentiates traditional tools and applications from so-called Knowledge Management tools

- Appreciate the technological infrastructure needed to support a successful Knowledge Management initiative

- Recognize the potential of disruptive information technologies to change the future of Knowledge Management

nowledge Management (KM) can be adopted as a strategy with little or no dependence on what's considered high tech today. The earliest knowledge workers did just fine with clay tablets of various shapes to archive and retrieve information for the local government. Similarly, communities of practice need little more than a physical space so that members can meet to discuss ideas. On a personal level, a chief executive officer (CEO) can do just fine without a personal digital assistant (PDA), relying, instead, on a notebook maintained by his or her assistant. Similarly, physicians, lawyers, and other knowledge workers don't need computer-based systems to do their work.

That said, Knowledge Management, like most other business strategies, *can* have more powerful results—as measured by the bottom line—with the appropriate use of information technology. As illustrated in Exhibit 5.1, the organic or unassisted approach contrasts significantly with the technologic approach based on computers, databases, and applications. Although there is considerable overlap in the two approaches, key differences are in the transaction volume ideal organization size, scalability, type of knowledge involved, and initial cost.

A technologic approach to Knowledge Management has a much higher initial cost, is inherently more scalable, and can handle a much greater transaction volume than an unassisted knowledge worker. For example, whereas an unaided customer service representative might be able to handle perhaps 1,000 customer complaints a month, a technology-enabled rep might be able to cover thousands of customer interactions per minute. Because of the leverage provided by technology, such as a software robot (bot) that interacts with customers over e-mail, the rep can work in an oversight capacity. The bot can handle most e-mail queries, supplying answers culled from past interactions with live customer service reps, and, on the rare occasions when the system can't adequately resolve a customer's issues, can pass the customer on to a live rep.

Technology in support of Knowledge Management isn't necessary or even optimal in every instance. For example, if the issues that have to be dealt with are subtle and require a very rich knowledge of the area, an expert knowledge worker or knowledge analyst may be the best option. Similarly, although technologies supportive of Knowledge Management can be applied successfully to organizations of any size, extensive investments in technology are generally practical only in medium-size to large companies. The organic approach is generally more practical for small to medium-size organizations.

From an implementation perspective, the key issues with a technologic approach are training the knowledge workers to use the technology appropriately and to use the appropriate controlled vocabulary. The organic approach, in contrast, necessarily focuses on the knowledge worker's skills in interacting with people and within retaining their knowledge in the organization.

Perhaps the most significant way technology enables the KM process is that it can provide virtual meeting space for communities of practice. Although a knowledge analyst or other knowledge worker can help organize a meeting, there is always the issue of meeting place, time, and other logistics. When collaborative technologies are available to provide

EXHIBIT 5.1

Technology versus Organic Knowledge Management

Focus	Technology	Organic
Enablers	Computers, databases, and applications	Knowledge workers
Human resources	Knowledge engineers	Knowledge analysts
Key issues	Vocabulary, training, knowledge workers	People skills, knowledge retention
Scalability	High	Low
Initial cost	High	Low
Ideal organization size	Small to large	Small to medium
Geographical constraints	None	Time zones, proximity limitations
Volume capacity	Thousands per minute	Thousands per month
Primary users	Customers, knowledge workers, managers, virtual communities of practice	Knowledge workers, high-end customers
Example company	Dell Computer	Hewlett-Packard
Applicability	Generic problems	Special cases
Knowledge required	Obvious, readily apparent, explicit	Rich, subtle, tacit

IN THE REAL WORLD

People versus Processors

Dell Computer allows customers to configure PCs with more than 40,000 combinations of hardware and software through its web site. Instead of dealing with an engineer or salesperson, customers interact directly with Dell's web site to compare prices and capabilities of various configurations. Although many customers then turn to the phone to actually place the order, the system saves Dell from having to train sales representatives on the continuous stream of new products and configurations.

The technology approach to Knowledge Management isn't a panacea, however. For example, even though it's a technology company, Hewlett-Packard relies heavily on the organic approach, using human knowledge workers in situations that require on-site, hands-on dissemination of information.

a virtual meeting, they can be held as frequently as necessary, for short periods, with no overhead of walking or traveling to a meeting place.

This chapter explores the many enabling technologies that can be applied to Knowledge Management at both the corporate level and the level of the individual knowledge worker. Before delving into a description of these and other enabling technologies, consider the challenges being addressed at the Custom Gene Factory.

Electronic Whiteboard

Like most other firms, Custom Gene Factory (CGF) is challenged with delivering an economically viable service to its customers in a highly competitive industry while investing heavily in new product development. As a result, the research and development department (R&D) is under pressure to develop new processes and communicate these ideas to production staff so that they can quickly move the most promising developments out of the laboratory and into trials with pharmaceutical firms. As such, the knowledge workers in the R&D department spend a great deal of time in ad hoc brainstorming sessions, where everyone associated with a project, in any department, comes up with as many unusual solutions as possible to move a product or process forward. However, because CGF's campus is spread out over six buildings and some of the pharmaceutical firm partners that are part of the community of practice are located in other cities, an unacceptably high overhead is associated with bringing the stakeholders together for regular meetings.

To facilitate the brainstorming sessions in a way that fits everyone's schedules, the chief knowledge officer (CKO) attends several of the meetings as an unobtrusive observer to determine the real needs of the

TIPS & TECHNIQUES

Suggest, Don't Tell

One of the basic principles of computer interface design is that the computer should be subservient to the human operator. When this principle is violated, operators, including highly educated knowledge workers, tend to be put off and, in some cases, threatened. The most successful decision-making programs respect human decision makers and merely suggest—don't tell—them what to do.

Perry Miller who developed the Critiquing system in the 1980s, was first to recognize the importance of allowing the human operator to feel in control of the decision-making process. The Critiquing system acts as a sounding board for organizing physicians' ideas, expressing agreement, or suggesting reasoned alternatives. This approach recognizes physicians' need to exercise control and places the computer in a subservient, nonthreatening role.

members. He discovers that the group relies heavily on the whiteboard, with the requisite note-taker who attempts to copy the contents of the board every few minutes. The meetings include multiple verbal exchanges, printed handouts, and the personal, face-to-face interchanges. Furthermore, at the start of every meeting, the group leader has to bring those who couldn't attend the previous meeting up to speed by reviewing the ideas offered and decisions made in their absence. Because of the scheduling problems, it's rare to have every stakeholder in the meeting at once, and some issues have to be discussed privately, further adding to the communications and time overhead for those involved in the meeting.

The CKO floats the idea of a computer-based collaborative system to the group. The ideal system would provide real-time video, voice, an electronic whiteboard, and text interchange with every member of the group. It also would keep a record of the exchanges arranged by date and topic. The group members agree to consider the options at the next meeting.

In the interim, the CKO consults with the chief information officer (CIO) to identify three software packages that are compatible with the corporate intranet, the pharmaceutical firms' networks, and the corporate hardware, and presents the options to the group. After a lengthy discussion, the group picks a solution. It's another month before the software and hardware upgrades—including desktop digital cameras—are installed and six weeks more for everyone to go through training. The first few meetings are less than ideal for those who enjoy the face-to-face interaction, but for everyone else, the system is a significant time-saver. With the collaborative system in place, everyone in the brainstorming group can attend the virtual meetings. Furthermore, everyone with access privileges can read through and add to the discussion asynchronously.

Issues

The work at CGF illustrates several issues regarding the use of technology to enable a KM program:

- Information technology can be critical in enabling KM processes. Numerous technologies are available to enable organizations to leverage their intellectual capital.

- Every technology initiative must involve the CIO or other representative of the information services (IS) group. Collaborative tools that involve sharing information between departments and especially between the company and external customers require compete cooperation with the IS department.

- Integrating technology into an organization takes time. Even though the collaborative technology paralleled a community of practice already in place at CGF, time was required for the IS department to install and test the hardware and software; participants needed training time; and finally, when the system was up and running, time was required to establish procedures for the group activity.

- It's how technology is used, not the technology's inherent capabilities, that define whether it's capable of enabling a KM program.

Enabling the Knowledge Management Process

The technologies available to enable the Knowledge Management process span the continuum from low-tech tools, such as pen and paper, to high-tech expert systems and virtual reality displays. For example, the telephone, tape recorders, whiteboards, and other technologies that most of us take for granted are enabling technologies in that they facilitate some aspects of the KM life cycle. However, when most people speak of enabling technologies, they're referring to more high-tech tools, such as PDAs, that provide some advantages over pen and paper. That distinction is a matter of degree and user experience. For example, in the late 1800s, the telephone switchboard was a disruptive technology that enabled business owners to collaborate with each other and their staff in real time over distances of several miles.

Exhibit 5.2 presents a wide range of enabling technologies, from authoring and decision support tools to controlled vocabularies and database tools, that can be used to enable various phases of the KM life cycle. In general, these technologies serve as intellectual levers that provide the connectivity needed to efficiently transfer information among knowledge workers, either in real time or asynchronously. In this regard, a database archive can be thought of as a storage area that adds a significant delay to the communications.

EXHIBIT 5.2

Life Cycle Phase	Primary Enabling Technologies
Creation/acquisition	Authoring tools, interface tools, data capture tools, decision support tools, simulations, professional databases, application-specific programs, database tools, pattern matching, groupware, controlled vocabularies, infrastructure, graphics tools
Modification	Authoring tools, decision support tools, infrastructure
Use	Interface tools, visualization tools, decision support tools, simulations, application-specific programs, database tools, pattern matching, groupware, infrastructure, web tools
Archiving	Database tools, cataloging tools, controlled vocabularies, infrastructure
Transfer	Groupware, infrastructure
Translation/repurposing	Decision support tools, simulations, database tools, infrastructure
Access	Interface tools, database tools, pattern matching, groupware, controlled vocabularies, infrastructure
Disposal	Database tools, infrastructure

Knowledge Management draws on technologies and approaches developed in virtually every field of computer science. For example, knowledge creation and acquisition benefit from technologies such as data mining, text summarizing, a variety of graphical tools, the use of intelligent agents, and a variety of information retrieval methodologies. Knowledge archiving and access benefit from information repositories and database tools. Knowledge use and transfer benefit from interface tools, intranets and internets, groupware, decision support tools, and collaborative systems. In addition, virtually all of the technologies involved in the KM life cycle assume an infrastructure capable of supporting moderate- to high-speed connectivity, security, and some degree of fault tolerance. The next sections describe the primary classes of enabling technologies listed in Exhibit 5.2 in more detail.

Groupware

Groupware typically is defined as any software that enables group collaboration over a network. Examples of groupware include shared authoring tools, electronic whiteboards, videoconferencing tools, online forums, e-mail, online screen sharing, and multimodal conferencing. Each of these technologies holds the potential to increase collaboration at a distance, reducing the cost of travel and the time knowledge workers waste in transit.

Shared authoring tools include common word processing programs, graphics programs, and sound editing utilities. Although they're not often sold as such, many stand-alone applications can be considered groupware if they can access and modify a document on the web or a common server. Most shared authoring tools must be used asynchronously, in that only one person at a time can make changes to a document.

E-mail systems that support asynchronous text-based communications are probably the most often used groupware. A related technology, online forums, is a real-time, text-based system that allows group posting and response to text messages. An online forum is self-archiving, in that the sequence of text-based conversations involving dozens or even hundreds of contributors is maintained for review by others. Instant messaging is an upcoming form of groupware that allows knowledge workers working away from their desks to exchange short packets of information. However, unlike online forums, the string of messages isn't stored automatically for future reference.

Screen sharing allows a user with the appropriate access privileges to connect to and take control of a remote PC. Screen sharing is especially popular in training and troubleshooting situations, where a support person can show the trainee at a remote site how to perform an operation and then watch as the trainee attempts to do the operation.

Even higher up the evolutionary ladder of groupware is the electronic whiteboard. This technology, expressly designed for group collaboration, provides a virtual whiteboard drawing space that enables multiple collaborators to take turns authoring and modifying hand-drawn graphics, highlighting points of interest on digital images, or simply posting a slide for a presentation. Whiteboards often are used in conjunction with other products, such as videoconferencing, the real-time, multi-way broadcasting of video and audio.

Because of network bandwidth limitations, videoconferencing often is configured to use the telephone lines for audio and the Internet or other network for the video channels. However, when the bandwidth is sufficient, many companies embrace multimodal conferencing to enable real-time collaboration. Multimodal conferencing represents the pinnacle of groupware, in that the technology supports real-time group sharing of an electronic whiteboard, a text forum, audio, and multiple-channel video.

As illustrated in Exhibit 5.3, groupware differs in responsiveness and the maximum number of simultaneous users that can be accommodated.

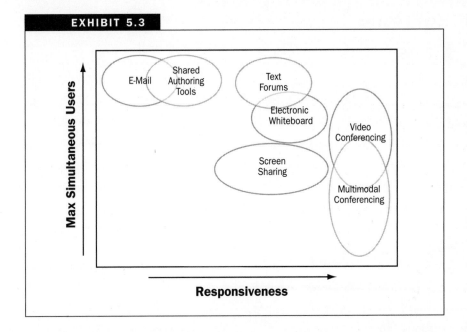

EXHIBIT 5.3

For example, an e-mail system can handle a virtually unlimited number of users, as long as they don't try to send e-mail at once. Also, users typically read and respond to e-mail at different times. In contrast, video-conferencing, which is real-time communication, supports a limited number of users because of limitations in the bandwidth of the network and the processing capacity of each user's PC.

Pattern Matching

Pattern matching, the major feature ascribed to programs in the field of artificial intelligence (AI), provides the foundation for many aspects of Knowledge Management. From a business perspective, the technology ideally enables a knowledge worker with relatively little experience to make decisions that otherwise would have required someone with much more experience. Examples of pattern matching applications in the realm of AI include expert systems, intelligent agents, and machine learning systems.

Expert Systems

Pattern matching is the basic technology underlying expert systems—programs that can make humanlike decisions, especially reasoning under conditions of uncertainty. Expert systems are also useful in helping experts work out a process, such as medical diagnosis. Once the process is distilled into rules, the logic can be incorporated into the standard programming environment or delivered as graphical decision diagram.

As an example of how pattern matching technology can be applied to Knowledge Management, consider the system illustrated in Exhibit 5.4. In this rule-based expert system, DecisionPro, by Vanguard Software,

EXHIBIT 5.4

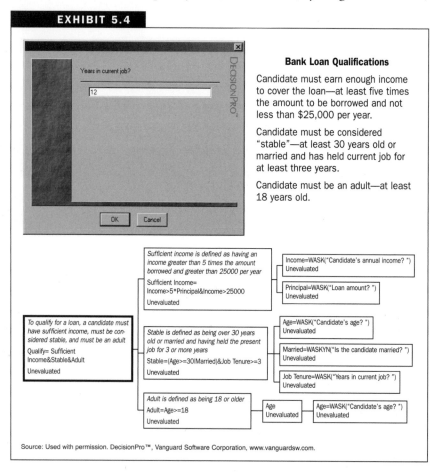

Bank Loan Qualifications

Candidate must earn enough income to cover the loan—at least five times the amount to be borrowed and not less than $25,000 per year.

Candidate must be considered "stable"—at least 30 years old or married and has held current job for at least three years.

Candidate must be an adult—at least 18 years old.

Source: Used with permission. DecisionPro™, Vanguard Software Corporation, www.vanguardsw.com.

Inc., rules are created in a decision tree format, as show at the bottom of the exhibit. The end user sees a simple sequence of questions (top left on the exhibit) and eventually is presented with a simple textual response.

Intelligent Agents

Intelligent agents, which are also known as bots or software robots, use pattern matching technology to do their work. Intelligent agents are especially significant in acquiring information from the web, commercial databases, and intranets or corporate intranets. Intelligent agents, which can be resident on a PC or web based, accept user questions, convert the questions into the appropriate language, and then submit the questions to the appropriate search engines. The intelligent agents then remove duplicates, place the results in a standard format, and rank order the results.

Most intelligent agents accept natural language input. The pattern matching technology that makes this possible is *natural language processing* (NLP). In addition to being useful in automatically formulating queries for search engines, NLP front ends can make database front ends more user friendly.

Database Tools

Databases, which provide a Knowledge Management system's long-term memory, have a variety of names, depending on their structure, contents, use, and amount of data they contain. Database tools form the basis for storing and retrieving business intelligence about what has happened in the company, which can then form the basis for future predictions. For example, a *data warehouse* is a central database, often very large, that can provide authorized users with access to all of a company's information. Data warehouses usually contain data from a variety of noncompatible sources.

On a much smaller scale is the *data mart*, an organized, searchable database system, organized according to the user's likely needs. Compared to a data warehouse, a data mart has a narrower focus on data that is specific to a particular workgroup or task. Both data warehouses and data marts typically are built with some form of *database management system*, which is a program that allows a knowledge worker to store, process, and manage data in a systematic way. A *data repository*, in contrast, is a database used as an information storage facility, with minimal analysis or querying functionality.

Fully functional data warehouses and data marts support *data mining* —the process of extracting meaningful relationships from usually very large quantities of seemingly unrelated data. Specialized data mining tools allow managers to perform competitive analysis, market segmentation, trend analysis, sensitivity analysis, and predictions based on information in the corporate database.

One of the requirements of data mining and archiving information in general is the availability of a controlled vocabulary. This controlled vocabulary is often implemented as a *data dictionary*—a translation program that maps or translates identical concepts that are expressed in different words or phrases into a single vocabulary.

Controlled Vocabularies

Creating information, archiving it for future uses, and communicating it to others and to computer systems is a formidable challenge. Not only must there be a common language and vocabulary, but there has to be a common taxonomy—a description of the relationship between words. From a business perspective, controlled vocabularies are critical because they define the ease with which knowledge workers and managers can store and retrieve information in Knowledge Management tools. Just as the best-stocked library or bookstore in the world isn't worth much if patrons or customers can't locate the information they need, the most complete corporate intelligence is useless without a means of identifying it for archiving and later retrieval.

A common contextual framework is mandatory in every successful KM initiative because words can have different meanings, depending on context and the perspectives of those involved. For example, the word "fish" may bring to mind a goldfish in a fish tank for a child, a marlin struggling on a line—that is, the action of fishing—for a fisherman, a plate with slab of seared salmon for an urban professional, or a box of frozen fish sticks for a college student.

Professional Databases

Professional or commercial databases and search engines contribute to the knowledge acquisition phase of virtually every knowledge organization. Organizations with access to these professional databases can save time and money that would otherwise be wasted on duplicating the effort involved in locating the information. In addition, the organization probably wouldn't meet the quality standards established by the companies offering professional databases. With access to the proper database and search tools, in-house expertise can be rapidly augmented with knowledge from outside sources. Dozens of fee-for-access databases exist that typically contain thousands of journal articles and industry-specific information.

Application-Specific Programs

The KM process typically is facilitated through groupware and other networked applications. However, hundreds of stand-alone, application-specific programs can be used in niche areas to save knowledge workers time and decrease errors. For example, there exist specialized, stand-alone applications designed to support the evaluation of employees, to balance a checkbook, to graph a process, or to privately brainstorm. The issues associated with using application-specific, stand-alone programs for Knowledge Management include having to learn multiple interfaces, duplication of data entry, and the associated errors.

Simulations

Perhaps the most powerful class of KM tools is simulation—programs that mimic reality by animating complex processes. Simulations are especially useful to convey complex relationships to a knowledge worker who has difficulty understanding to tables of numbers or equations. Simulations are an excellent means of exploring what-if scenarios in an interactive format because they can display complex processes in an easy-to-understand way.

Consider how the simulation package Extend, from Imagine That, Inc., shown in Exhibit 5.5, allows the observer to view and manipulate the parameters involved in determining the staffing and equipment requirements for a hamburger stand. The user can manipulate the process in the kitchen and observe the effect on customer wait time. By aiding in visualization, simulations increase the odds that the user will comprehend more of the subtle relationships in a process, compared to a simple table of data or equations.

Decision Support Tools

Decision support tools are software tools that allow managers and other knowledge workers to make decisions by reviewing and manipulating the data stored on a PDA, on one extreme, to a data warehouse, on the other. Many of the technologies discussed here can be applied to some form of decision support.

Decision support tools are one way to disseminate best practices, using technologies such as expert systems, simulations, and statistical

EXHIBIT 5.5

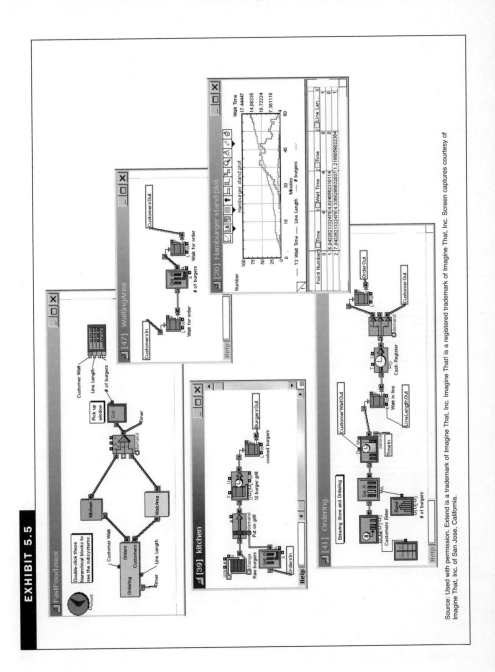

Source: Used with permission. Extend is a trademark of Imagine That, Inc. Imagine That! is a registered trademark of Imagine That, Inc. Screen captures courtesy of Imagine That, Inc. of San Jose, California.

analysis tools to view or manipulate information stored in the corporate data warehouse. These tools include text summarizing utilities—programs that distill a paragraph from extensive documents—outline generators, statistical programs to analyze data, and decision tables to verify that every possible scenario has been considered.

Data Capture Tools

Data capture—getting information accurately and efficiently into a machine-readable form, whether a payroll total or the notes from the latest community of practice meeting—is typically the most challenging part of a Knowledge Management initiative. Even if knowledge workers and experts are willing to contribute their rules and heuristics to the corporate data warehouse, there is the issue of capturing the information efficiently and accurately. However, a KM initiative can't be expected to improve the company's bottom line without information.

In general, the technologies used for data capture are defined by the source. On the web, for example, public search engines form the basis for data capture. For printed material in the office, optical character recognition (OCR) technologies, from flatbed scanners to hand-held wands, can be used to convert printed text to machine-readable text. Whiteboard recorders and digital cameras can save error-prone transcription from traditional whiteboards. Similarly, tape recorders can be used to capture voice for either manual or automatic (voice recognition) transcription later.

Besides working with text, speech, and images, data capture technologies can be applied to physical objects. Bar codes allow rapid tracking of inventory, for example. Similarly, real-time location sensors support object tracking—whether what is tracked is knowledge workers in a factory or widgets on an assembly line.

Visualization Tools

A slide presentation with histograms and other images is usually much more appreciated and effective than a text presentation on the same subject. Graphics and animations, when appropriately rendered, can decrease the time required for knowledge workers to grasp complex processes and allow nonexperts to verify the accuracy of relationships that would have been unwieldy to describe with tables of data.

Simulation-based animations are especially good at imparting the dynamic relationship between variables. Examples of visualization tools range from three-dimensional graphic packages to simple pie chart and histogram output from spreadsheets and other traditional office programs.

Interface Tools

Getting information out of a database is as important as acquiring it. The point of human-computer communication—the interface—defines the quality and efficiency of the interchange. The better the interface, the easier it is for knowledge workers and managers to interact with computer-based tools. In addition to a mouse, keyboard, speakers, and video display, a variety of specialized software and hardware can make the user interface more effective.

For example, text-to-speech (TTS) engines are useful in creating speech from text displayed on the screen. TTS is commonly used in conjunction with avatars, or graphical representations of some part of the computer, information in the data warehouse, or another knowledge worker. The Microsoft Office "Paper Clip" is one example of how an avatar can be used to introduce novice users to word processing with a computer program. A more warmly accepted avatar is Ananova, the first virtual newscaster (*www.ananova.com*).

Authoring Tools

Creating information is integral to virtually every knowledge worker's duty in a knowledge organization. However, the less time spent authoring, the more time knowledge workers and managers have to do other work. Authoring tool technology has progressed rapidly since the introduction of the first word processing programs. Today multimedia editors are used almost as often as text editors are for creating content. Graphics programs are available for creating print documents and for projecting to an audience, image editors for rendering web-friendly photographs and animations. Similarly, sound editors for creating sound effects or editing speech and video editing systems for preparing video for presentation over the web or the corporate intranet are readily available, affordable, and applicable to the information authoring process.

Infrastructure

All of the above technologies—and all of their potential business advantages—assume some form of information infrastructure, which minimally involves a computer platform or image-capture hardware of some type, from desktop PCs, to laptops, hand-helds, and cell phones. The infrastructure also includes the information storage media, from magnetic tape and floppy disks to hard drives, CD-ROMs, and DVDs. These infrastructure technologies can either add to or take away from the bottom line, depending on how they are implemented and the synergies that exist between infrastructure and the technologies it supports.

Groupware relies on a high-speed network connection among knowledge workers and between knowledge workers and computer systems. The network can take the form of the Internet and the web, intranets, and internets, including their associated cables, servers, and network operating system software, and browsers. Wireless systems obviate the need for cables but introduce additional issues, such as the need for increased security.

The security infrastructure may include the use of biometrics and other authentication systems, encryption, use tracking, and digital rights management software to verify that copyright holders' rights haven't been violated. With the melding of voice and data in most of corporate America, the telecommunications infrastructure is taking on increasing significance in supporting traditional phone and teleconferencing.

On the Horizon

The technologies most likely to have a significant impact on Knowledge Management soon deal with systems integration, the process in which different computer applications and systems are connected so that they can share data. Since the applications in a typical corporation often are cobbled together from different vendors, purchased years apart, and running on different hardware, system integration is usually a custom programming task. As a result, system integration can take months of effort, considerable expense, and have only mixed results. An alternative to integrating one or more applications into an existing infrastructure is to purchase an integrated set of tools, commonly marketed as content management software and hardware.

The most promising technologies in the system integration arena are *Web services* and *Application Service Provider (ASP)* tools. Web services involve the use of the Web to provide a standard means of sharing data between applications, whereas ASP technology provides knowledge workers with access to software through a Web browser, negating the need for corporation to purchase and run copies of the software locally. This reliance on the Internet and other networks is increasingly common, as in outsourcing storage through Internet-based storage area networks and storage service providers instead of purchasing huge servers in-house. These technologies provide virtually unlimited storage as part of huge server farms that may be located across the country or in another country.

Numerous technologies can have the potential to aid in capturing information from experts, from neural networks to genetic programming. These technologies hold some promise for the future of Knowledge Management. In addition, several companies are experimenting with smart workplaces, where sensors determine the physical location of a knowledge worker, changing information displays to suit the user's preconfigured preferences and adjusting the information access level accordingly. From a hardware perspective, tablet PCs, wearable PCs, and PDAs are likely to continue to increase in functionality and applicability to Knowledge Management, especially as they relate to the car-based office (telematics).

Clearly, the most significant challenge surrounding the effective use of KM technology is integration—not at the software or hardware level, but with the user. For example, decision support tools should be transparent to the current workflow, thereby augmenting current processes and contributing to the bottom line. The challenge on the horizon isn't in the hardware or software but work standards and processes. For example, digital rights management software—software that decides who can see a file by appending access rights to a document—is useless without standards for authenticating and authorizing users for reading, modifying, or printing files.

Summary

Knowledge Management, as a business strategy, is independent of technology. However, the appropriate technology, applied judiciously to the proper phase of the K life cycle, can significantly improve the efficiency and effectiveness of the KM process. Although there are no shrink-wrapped KM tools per se, virtually any information technology can be useful at some phase of the KM life cycle. Some technologies, such as groupware, are especially attractive as potential enablers for the KM process.

As in the general information technology industry, the challenges on the horizon are predominantly related to integration, both at the systems level and at the human-computer interface. In this regard, technologies that fit seamlessly and unobtrusively with the workflow of knowledge workers and managers hold the greatest potential for enabling the business of Knowledge Management.

When you are inspired by some great purpose, some extraordinary project, all your thoughts break their bonds; your mind transcends limitations, your consciousness expands in every direction, and you find yourself in a new, great and wonderful world.

—Patanjali

CHAPTER 6

Solutions

After reading this chapter you will be able to

- Evaluate the technology solutions that can potentially enable the Knowledge Management process

- Appreciate the power of the request for proposal in gathering information internally and in specifying and evaluating the solutions offered by vendors

- Establish criteria for evaluating developers and vendors in the Knowledge Management market

Identifying technologies that potentially can support a Knowledge Management (KM) initiative is complicated because the definition of Knowledge Management is often a matter of perspective. To senior management of a large corporation, Knowledge Management is a strategy that promises to help increase the organization's competitiveness and improve its bottom line. To established technology vendors offering products in related fields, Knowledge Management represents an untapped opportunity for repurposed products and services. Similarly, to vendors with original technologies focused on enabling Knowledge Management, the market is an opportunity to introduce their innovative technologies and novel combinations of traditional information technologies. To the marketing arms of these companies, databases suddenly become "knowledge bases," text outline editors become "thought processors," and database and data mining tools become integral components of "content management" suites.

However, even technically savvy chief information officers (CIOs), chief knowledge officers (CKOs), and other senior managers know that evaluating a potential KM solution goes far beyond understanding the technology. At least as important are the developer's commitment to staying in the KM niche, the challenges of integrating technologies of any type into the corporate culture, and the degree to which the vendor will be of assistance in moving a KM initiative forward in the corporation. Of course, determining whether the corporation can afford the solution, considering both the short-term investment and the expected long-term return on investment (ROI), can override all other decisions. These and other economic considerations are covered in Chapter 7.

This chapter explores how the various enabling technologies can be identified and evaluated as potential solutions for a corporation's KM initiatives. It focuses on the information-gathering phase of an implementation, before a decision has been made to fully commit to a particular technology or approach. To illustrate some of the methods available to assess Knowledge Management solutions, let's return to Custom Gene Factory.

Formulating a Strategy

Up to now, most of the Knowledge Management activities in the Custom Gene Factory (CGF) have been tactical and focused on specific tasks. There is a company-wide collaborative system in place, for example, that provides an electronic whiteboard and text interchange to support virtual, impromptu meetings for communities of practice. However, there is no corporate-wide strategy for indexing, archiving, and disseminating the information recorded by the system and no integration of the collaborative system with other information systems in the corporation.

Working closely with a team of senior managers, middle managers, and representatives from various communities of practice, the CKO crafts a request for proposal (RFP) that reflects a consensus on what types of technologies are needed to move KM practices in the corporation to the next level. The CKO then mails the RFP describing the ideal content management system to the top content management vendors based on published rankings and magazine advertisements. The CKO also posts notices of the RFP on the company's web site and on several of the online KM newsgroups.

About three months later, at the proposal deadline, the CKO and other team members who contributed to the RFP read the dozen proposals in hand. They create a short list of developers and vendors that seem most likely to succeed in the field, based on reputation, client base, and references. Products from the selected vendors and developers are evaluated in terms of the potential synergies between the current KM process and their fit with CGF's culture. Since CGF's culture is relatively open and unconstrained, proposals that describe content management systems that impose a strict control hierarchy over the KM processes are avoided in favor of solutions that allow flexibility in control.

Vendors and developers also are evaluated from a business perspective, on issues such as price, functionality, likely ROI, and compatibility with the current information system infrastructure. An overall risk score is assigned to the top three solutions, and the composite analysis of each solution is graphed to highlight the relative strengths and weaknesses of each vendor's proposal (see Exhibit 6.1).

As a result of the comparative analysis, including the risk to CGF in the event of vendor failure, investing in the wrong hardware and/or software standards, or investing in a solution that proves to be unworkable, senior management decides that the risk is too great to implement a company-wide KM system in one step. Instead, management elects to

EXHIBIT 6.1

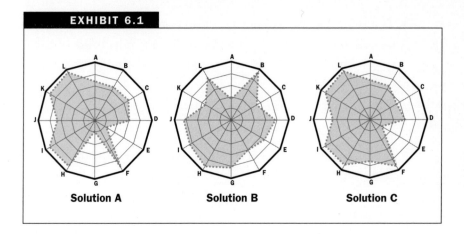

Solution A   Solution B   Solution C

run a limited pilot program with the top vendor. A contract is negoti-ated. Within three months, the pilot content management suite is installed in the company's research and development (R&D) division. The challenge before the CKO, management of the R&D division, and the vendor is applying the technology in a way that demonstrates a measurable ROI.

Issues

The steps CGF undertakes that result in the pilot program illustrate sev-eral key issues associated with identifying and evaluating potential KM solutions:

- The selection process begins with looking inside the organiza-tion to determine needs, not looking to vendors for solutions.

- The driving force for collecting information within the organization is the creation of a request for proposal, a working document that specifies the functional and technical requirements of the technology solution to the current KM challenges facing the corporation. Because the RFP is drafted collaboratively, it represents a consensus of opinion inside the organization.

- The RFP specifies vendor selection criteria. These typically include infrastructure requirements, price, product functionality, vendor and developer reputation, and the fit of technology with corporate culture.

- The company's CIO or technically competent CKO must be involved in selecting a solution.

- A technical KM solution not only enables the existing KM processes and workflow of the organization but fits the organization's culture. Therefore, potential solutions must be evaluated on nontechnical, functional issues as well as technical merits.

Evaluation Process

The story of Custom Gene Factory's quest for an enterprise-wide Knowledge Management solution illustrates the process of evaluating the merits and cost of technologies that can support a KM initiative. Although some stages often are performed in parallel, the solution evaluation process is best appreciated as a serial process, as diagrammed in Exhibit 6.2.

The process of enabling a KM program with technology involves nine stages:

1. Determine the needs of the organization.
2. Establish a budget.
3. Develop a request for proposal.
4. Issue the RFP.
5. Assess the proposals from vendors.
6. Evaluate the potential solutions.
7. Negotiate a contract with the vendor of choice.
8. Work with the vendor to implement the solution.
9. Assess the results.

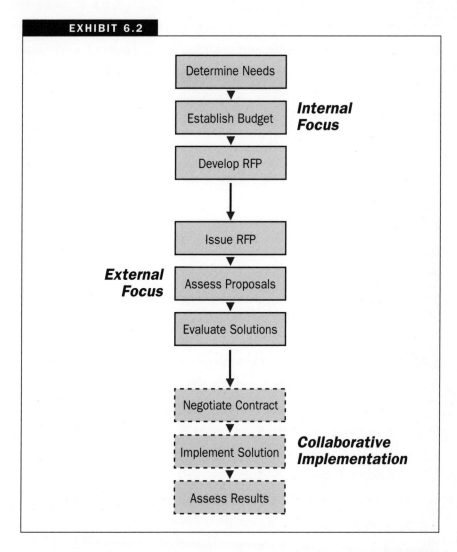

EXHIBIT 6.2

For the purpose of identifying and assessing potential technology-based solutions to KM challenges, the first six stages of the implementation process are the most critical. Therefore, the discussion here focuses on those stages. The last three stages, which involve the actual implementation of the solution, are covered in Chapter 8.

The first three stages in the process, which culminate in an RFP, are primarily internally focused. As in the story of CGF, creating a meaningful RFP requires consensus among management and knowledge workers in the organization regarding what constitutes an ideal technical solution to the current KM challenges. The next three stages, leading to the identification of the best solution available that satisfies the constraints defined in the RFP, are primarily externally focused. They involve focusing not only on the technology but on the developer and vendor. A technologically superior product from a developer with an unrealistic business model or poor reputation is a high-risk investment.

Determine the Needs of the Organization

In the story of CGF, the technical needs of the organization become apparent to the senior management as the knowledge workers and management became familiar with how technology can support and enhance existing KM processes.

Similarly, a corporation faced with choosing its KM technology should look to current KM practices and how technology can be used to enable them. In addition, simply because a KM process is being performed with, for example, the aid of a meeting room with wall-to-wall whiteboards and a refrigerator full of soft drinks doesn't mean that moving to a computer-based system will improve on the effectiveness of communities of practice. Working collaboratively in the same space creates a certain group dynamic. Thus, the meeting room, designated for meetings of communities of practice, may be more valuable to the organization than a new videoconferencing system or electronic whiteboard. That's where the expertise and knowledge of a CKO comes into play—recognizing which KM processes should be technology enabled and which ones are best left alone. Only then can he or she find the most appropriate technological solutions for a given KM challenge. Examples of situations in a knowledge organization that suggest an enabling technology may be able to improve on the effectiveness of—or extend the reach of—current KM practices include rapid growth, geographical expansion, and feedback from knowledge workers that the current infrastructure isn't supportive of their KM efforts.

The potential downside of driving a cultural change through the introduction of an enabling technology is that the amount of time from when the early adopters start using the technology to when laggards embrace the technology can span several years. For example, when e-mail was first introduced into a large organization, it typically took several years for everyone to come online. There are exceptions, of course, as when senior management dictates that paper memos are no longer allowed. However, it's impossible for management to dictate the formation of communities of practice and expect them to produce meaningful results. The easiest, quickest path to Knowledge Management is when technology follows and enables established KM practices.

Establishing a Budget

Establishing a budget for a minor or even a major Knowledge Management initiative typically isn't as challenging as actually obtaining the funds for the project. However, when faced with coming up with a reasonable budget, the best approach is to consult with companies of roughly the same size and scope in the same field that have installed KM technologies. Another approach is to hire a consultant with the requisite experience in KM technologies. However, when a consultant is used, the issue becomes one of locating someone who isn't wedded to a particular vendor or approach.

From a practical perspective, the incremental cost of implementing a corporate-wide KM initiative varies from about $100 to $6,000 or more per seat for software alone. A major component of the cost is the infrastructure, including the underlying network, support hardware and software, and desktop or hand-held systems. The incremental cost reflects the expense of software licenses, hardware upgrades, and training.

Develop the Request for Proposal

The most important internal step to take in identifying a technologic solution to enabling Knowledge Management in the organization is to establish exactly what management and knowledge workers need to support an ongoing or planned KM initiative. In this regard, the RFP encompasses not only the minimum technical requirements for a technology but instructs the vendor how it can meet and exceed corporate expectations. For the knowledge organization, an RFP is an internal working document that serves as a sounding board for all internal stakeholders involved in the KM effort. The RFP forces those involved in the initiative to consider the benefits that they expect the system to deliver—

 TIPS & TECHNIQUES

Multifunctional Request for Proposal

For a company not certain of the options available in the Knowledge Management market, investing the time to craft an RFP that describes the corporate environment can pay for itself many times over in consulting time, lost time on the job, and travel expenses. Senior managers or company representatives won't have to waste time at KM trade shows and meeting with vendors, instead vendors will beat a path to the company to point out how their products can be applied to company's current KM processes. Competing vendors are more than happy to point out faults and gaps in the competition's offerings, and provide industry-wide pricing norms, references, and other information that otherwise the company would have to pay to acquire. Although the practice of using vendors as free consultants may not be completely fair to vendors, it's an excellent starting point for a company serious about acquiring technology to enable its KM activities.

the *requirements specifications*—as well as the technical, detailed specifications that the system must conform to—the *functional specifications*.

The requirements specifications are qualitative descriptions of the expectations of knowledge workers and managers. For example, a statement such as "The system will provide our knowledge workers with the ability to communicate using audio, video, and text, in real time, over our existing network system" could appear as part of the requirements specifications of the RFP. Exactly how this expectation is met is the challenge that vendors must address to win the corporation's business. However, rarely are vendors completely free to devise a solution without several technical constraints—as defined by the functional specifications. The functional specification for the real-time audio, video, and text communications system could define, in explicit technical terms, the quality and bandwidth of the audio, video, and text; exactly what "real time" means; and could provide a technical definition of the network constraints.

The functional requirements are listed in the RFP so that vendors know what the corporation has in mind and senior management is in agreement regarding what a vendor is expected to deliver. The corporation's objective evaluation criteria, such as the contribution of up-front costs and the use of subcontractors added to the vendor's estimate, provides an overall evaluation score that gives vendors a clear idea of where they need to be in order to be competitive. Internally, the objective evaluation criteria listed in the RFP are helpful in overcoming personal biases and emotional attachments to a particular vendor during the evaluation of proposals.

Issue the Request for Proposal

There are several ways to issue an RFP. The first is to use a shotgun approach, using a variety of print media and the web to invite vendors to contact the corporation for a copy of the RFP. This nonspecific approach has the advantage of attracting vendors that would otherwise be unknown to the corporation. The disadvantages are that some major vendors in the Knowledge Management market may not take notice of the RFP and that the corporation may be inundated with time-wasting, generic proposals that don't address its specific needs.

A second approach is to target specific vendors, based on the advice of a consultant, the results of a web or magazine search, or by interviewing several experts in the KM field. The advantage of a targeted approach is that vendors contacted directly are more likely to respond in a way that addresses the RFP.

One challenge in using the directed approach to issuing RFPs is that vendors must be identified for each class of tools required. As shown in Exhibit 6.3, certain companies specialize in a variety of KM products as well as general, industry-standard products can be used for Knowledge Management. In identifying specific technology vendors, the experiences of the CIO and CKO are particularly relevant. For example, every CIO will have experience with or at least be familiar with standard database products from Microsoft, Oracle, Sybase, IBM, MySQL AB, and InterSystems.

Another approach, as illustrated in the story of the Custom Gene Factory, is to use a combination of shotgun and directed approaches. The downside of this hybrid approach is that a potentially large number of proposals may have to be evaluated very carefully.

Assess the Proposals

As the deadline specified in the RFP nears, proposals from vendors will begin filtering in. In assessing these proposals, it's tempting to turn first to the solution and ignore the peripheral information that has a direct bearing on it—information on the vendor and the developers of the

EXHIBIT 6.3

Technologies	Example Companies
Content management	Autonomy, BroadVision, Citrix, Documentum, Epicentric, FatWire, Hummingbird, IBM, Merant, Microsoft, Open Text, Oracle, Plumtree, SAP, Stellent, Teltech Resource Network
Data mining	Brio Technology, Cognos, Crystal Decisions, Microstrategy, IBM
Database management systems	Microsoft, Oracle, Sybase, IBM, MySQL AB, InterSystems
Digital rights management	HP, Xerox, Microsoft, Sun Microsystems
Expert systems	Vanguard Software, Tacit Knowledge Systems, NEC
Intelligent agents (desktop)	Intelliseek, Copernic, Lexibot, WebFerret, SearchPad, WebStorm, NetAttache
Intelligent agents (web)	Dogpile, Ixquick, MetaCrawler, QbSearch, ProFusion, SurfWax, Vivisimo
Interenterprise computing	SAP, i2 Technologies, Manugistics, Ariba, Commerce One, Oracle
Intracorporation search engines	AskMe, Cadenza
Professional databases	LexisNexis, Factiva, OCLC Online Computer Library Center, Inc., RocketNews, Dialog, InfoTrac, EBSCO Online, SkyMinder, ProQuest, Intelliseek, Scirus, Softbase, Ingenta
Public search engines	Google, Lycos, Yahoo!, Excite, AltaVista, AllTheWeb, CompletePlanet
Real time collaboration	TeraGlobal, Groove Networks, Lotus, Divine
Simulation systems	Imagine That!, Decision Engineering, Promodel, Production Modeling, Simul8
Visualization	The Brain Technologies, SAS, Minitab, Advanced Visual Systems

technology discussed. Any vendor can claim to provide solutions with virtually unlimited functionality—either because the vendor doesn't understand the RFP or because it wants the business so badly that it will agree to anything. For this reason, the first two items to be assessed in the proposal should be the vendor and developer. Consider the information on the products and services promised only if the vendors and developers fulfill established criteria.

As illustrated in Exhibit 6.4, assessment of developers and vendors involves consideration of unique features and many common elements. For example, in assessing a developer, a key issue is provision for future products. Some developers have a single product that hasn't been upgraded in years, except for slight modifications to make it compatible with operating system upgrades. Other developers have a vision for future feature sets, integration with other systems, and increased functionality. These forward-looking developers are generally more likely to be around in three to five years than developers content to milk current offerings.

EXHIBIT 6.4

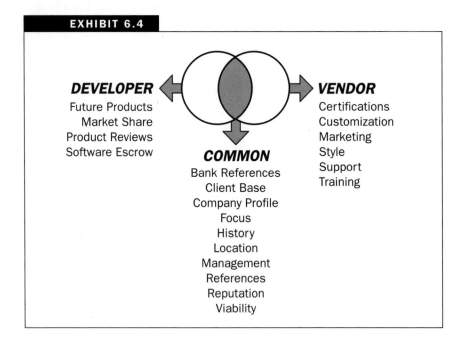

DEVELOPER
Future Products
Market Share
Product Reviews
Software Escrow

VENDOR
Certifications
Customization
Marketing
Style
Support
Training

COMMON
Bank References
Client Base
Company Profile
Focus
History
Location
Management
References
Reputation
Viability

Another developer issue is market share, in that it's safer to go with a developer that controls a significant share of its market. Product reviews, especially independent reviews in magazines or journals, are another source of information about developers and their products. They should be consistently positive. The willingness of a developer to provide a software escrow is also a critical assessment factor. Software escrow can lessen the likelihood that a developer will leave the corporation stranded with a dead-end product if the development effort fails or falls behind the development schedule.

A major vendor-specific evaluation criterion is whether a vendor is developer certified. Not only should vendors be certified by the developers they represent, but the certification must be meaningful. It should represent, for example, the fact that the vendor regularly receives training on the specific product. Lack of official certification may mean that the vendor either didn't take the time to attend the requisite classes or failed the certification process. Certification is especially relevant when the solution must be customized to fit the corporation's needs. Customization performed by a noncertified vendor may not be supported by the developer.

The availability of the vendor for internal marketing efforts may be critical for a successful implementation. Integrating a Knowledge Management product into an organization involves much more than simply installing a software package and plugging in the associated hardware. It takes a concerted internal corporate marketing effort to achieve buy-in from the knowledge workers and managers the technology is intended to empower. Vendors should be ready and willing assist with the buy-in process by participating in an official kickoff event and by providing management and knowledge workers with additional information. For example, vendors should be prepared to share successes stories and, more important, accounts of failures in similar companies.

IN THE REAL WORLD

Technology Disconnect

In evaluating the ability of technology to enable or amplify an existing or nascent KM initiative, it's easy to lose sight of the underlying premise of Knowledge Management. As defined in Chapter 1, Knowledge Management is a deliberate, systematic business optimization strategy that selects, distills, stores, organizes, packages, and communicates information essential to the business of a company in a manner that improves employee performance and corporate competitiveness. However, it's possible to technology-enable a process that performs superbly at improving employee performance, for example, but doesn't improve the bottom line. In other words, it's possible to have a disconnect between what is viewed as sharing, communications, and Knowledge Management, and the business of making money.

For example, Xerox's Palo Alto Research Center (PARC), the advanced R&D center created by Xerox in 1970, has a reputation for excellent R&D, work environment, sharing, and Knowledge Management—but no business sense. As in many companies with innovative R&D divisions, PARC traditionally has failed to fully capitalize on its innovations, leaving other companies to reap the business rewards for its work.

One lesson that can be learned from the PARC experience is that management shouldn't limit its activities to enabling communities of practice, virtual collaborations, and other KM activities. It must ensure that the information and innovations developed in these groups don't stay within the confines of R&D but are communicated to those who can take innovations and successfully bring them to market.

A vendor's style has to mesh with the company culture if management is to get buy-in from internal knowledge workers. A compatible style is also necessary for effective training and support. For example, a vendor with a laidback approach may be incompatible with high-powered knowledge workers who value their time above all else. For these workers, a vendor with a slow, methodical, and complete style of teaching and product support may be intolerable.

Many vendors and developers work in concert with a client. For example, the vendor may provide sales and account management, while the developer provides training and ongoing support. The common factors related to vendor and developer assessment focus on parameters that define the business relationship and the likelihood that the vendor and developers will continue to exist in the long term. Bank references regarding financial status, breadth and depth of the client base, and management structure and experience are good indicators of vendor and developer stability.

The reputations of the vendor and the developer, references, and history provide a subjective measure of what the company can expect in terms of adhering to time lines, cost, and service. Finally, location may be a practical concern, especially the relative location of the vendor. Off-site training at the vendor's facilities is much less expensive when the vendor is local. Similarly, it's a bonus to be able to drop by the developer's main offices to discuss product issues. At the other extreme, developers located overseas often present a considerable risk, even when there is a local vendor. If the developer folds, enforcing contractual obligations may be impractical.

Evaluate the Technology Solutions

With the proposals from viable vendors and developers in hand, the next step is to evaluate the technology solutions. This phase of the evaluation process involves obtaining hands-on experience with the product. To this end, most vendors of shrink-wrapped software solutions will agree to a 30-day free trial. For more complicated systems that require some degree of customization or special hardware, many vendors will agree to absorb some of the cost of a pilot program in which a limited installation is provided for a three- or four-month trial.

The KM-specific criteria for evaluating solutions are a function of the product. Assuming a software application aimed at enabling communities of practice, potential criteria include:

- *Compatibility.* The product should be compatible with the operating system used, third-party KM programs, and legacy systems.

- *Support.* Product support should include official user's groups, vendor or developer newsletters, and official publications.

- *Synergy.* The product should support for processes within the organization that enable ongoing communities of practice.

- *Performance.* The effectiveness and efficiency with which the product supports activities within communities of practice should be a performance standard.

In the end, the features and benefits of every solution have to be evaluated in terms of price. In this evaluation, it's important to distinguish between the initial purchase price and ongoing, long-term costs. Besides the purchase price, there is the cost of maintenance—typically 30 percent of the original price per year. Ongoing license fees, can range from 10 to 20 percent of the purchase price annually. The cost of upgrades should be evaluated if they aren't covered in the maintenance contract.

Solutions should be evaluated in terms of indirect costs that are usually not included in the contract with the vendor. For example, if the system is intended to support real-time video conferencing over the web, the buying organization may need to upgrade its current network hardware and software and purchase additional peripherals, such as larger monitors, digital video cameras, and speakers.

Negotiate the Contract

After a thorough evaluation of the proposals, the next step is to negotiate a contract with the top vendor. As noted earlier, since a vendor's response to an RFP isn't legally binding, it's prudent to fold the original RFP and the vendor's proposal into the final contract. Negotiation and the next two phases of the implementation process are covered in more detail in Chapter 8.

Implement the Solution

Implementation is usually a shared activity that requires resources from the vendor, the developer, and the organization. Details of the implementation that should be specified exactly in the negotiated contract include the time line, deliverables, the sign-off procedure, and means of resolving disputes.

Assess Results

Assessing the results of an implementation involves comparing the functional and requirements specifications with what is delivered as well as evaluating the overall effect on the organization, especially the bottom line. Chapter 8 continues the discussion of Knowledge Management from the perspective of the numerous stakeholders involved in a KM initiative and the likely return on investment.

Summary

Technologic solutions to Knowledge Management can be evaluated as part of a nine-phase process that revolves around the RFP. Inside the corporation, the RFP serves as a working document that management and knowledge workers can use to specify their KM needs. For vendors, the RFP serves as the basis for their responses. The RFP also provides the knowledge organization with a standard with which proposals can be evaluated objectively. Finally, the RFP and the top vendor's proposal are folded into the negotiated contract to make the vendor's responses legally binding. In searching for a technologic solution to KM challenges, the RFP is central to setting expectations both within the organization and with the selected vendors and developers that will implement the solution.

Do not believe what you have heard.

Do not believe in tradition because it is handed down many generations.

Do not believe in anything that has been spoken of many times.

Do not believe because the written statements come from some old sage.

Do not believe in conjecture.

Do not believe in authority or teachers or elders.

But after careful observation and analysis, when it agrees with reason and it will benefit one and all, then accept it and live by it.

—Buddha

CHAPTER 7

Economics

After reading this chapter you will be able to

- Appreciate the economic value of Knowledge Management to knowledge workers, managers, customers, and other major stakeholders

- Appreciate the economic risks associated with a Knowledge Management initiative

- Understand the methods of assessing the economic contribution of intangibles to corporate value

Enacting change in the corporate environment, while often necessary, is always expensive. Overcoming the inertia of corporate culture, especially in larger corporations, takes time, energy, and money. For this reason, any change has to have not only a reasonable return on investment (ROI), but excellent odds of succeeding in the corporate environment. The business landscape is littered with carcasses of companies whose well-meaning management went down the reengineering path, only to find that change was more expensive than they anticipated and the ROI was either insignificant or nonexistent.

In considering a Knowledge Management (KM) initiative, a corporation's senior management has to answer several basic questions:

- Will Knowledge Management save the corporation money?

- Will it generate extra revenue?
- If so, how long will it take, and what resources will have to be invested?
- What's the downside of a failed initiative?

If, after two or three years, there isn't a real, demonstrable change in the corporate bottom line, all other considerations are secondary. One of the major challenges of working in the intangible world of Knowledge Management is defining exactly what constitutes the bottom line. Traditional measurement tools, such as an ROI calculation, fail to adequately consider many of the positive, qualitative contributions ascribed to Knowledge Management.

One reason that ROI measurements fail in evaluating the effect of Knowledge Management on the bottom line is that many of the effects are qualitative and difficult to measure, such as an increase in the number of communities of practice. For example, consider the potential benefits of a KM program listed in Exhibit 7.1. The quantitative benefits, such as cost savings, increased stock valuation, and reduced cost of sales can be evaluated objectively, but the qualitative benefits, such as increased customer loyalty, positive cultural change, and employee empowerment, are difficult to assess or apply metrics to, especially in the short term.

Consider the challenge of measuring the potential benefit of increased innovation. The first challenge is defining exactly what "increased innovation" signifies. For example, is the metric an increased *rate* of innovation, an increased *quality* of innovation, or an increased *number* of innovations in a given area? Furthermore, what constitutes an innovation? In the long-term, "increased innovation" could be expected to result in quantifiable outcomes, such as an increased number of patent applications or patents, more white papers in the company library, more

---

EXHIBIT 7.1

Potential Benefits of Knowledge Management

Quantitative	Qualitative
Cost savings	Better management of ideas
Greater customer acquisition rate	Decreased likelihood employee defection
Improved bottom line	
Improved profit margins	Greater customer loyalty
Increased corporate valuation	Increased collaboration with customers
Increased customer loyalty behavior	
Increased customer retention	Increased customer satisfaction
Increased market share	Increased innovation
Increased repeat purchases	Increased knowledge worker empowerment
Increased stock valuation	
Reduced cost of sales	Increased knowledge worker productivity
	Increased knowledge worker satisfaction
	Increased market leadership
	Increased organizational stability
	Increased shareholder satisfaction
	Increased understanding of customer needs
	Positive cultural change

---

published articles in the trade magazines authored by knowledge workers and managers, or more national awards for innovation.

A related issue is proving causality instead of mere correlation. Simply because a company produces patent applications at a higher rate two or three years following the implementation of a KM program isn't proof of causality. The increased rate of applications could have come from a new hire who is particularly innovative, unusually prolific, and very creative—and who doesn't even use the new KM system.

Furthermore, in the short term—a year or two into a KM project—there isn't likely to be any direct measures of increased innovation. Only indirect measures, such as an increase in the number of communities of practice, may indicate increased innovation in the organization. However, there's no hard evidence that increased innovation results from more frequent or technology-enhanced community of practice meetings.

Some qualitative measures are more directly linked to quantitative outcome measures than others. For example, "greater customer loyalty" eventually should be reflected in loyalty behavior, such as increased repeat business and customer retention. However, even in these cases, at best the relationship between short-term qualitative assessment and longer-term quantitative ones is correlative, not causal. Increased customer retention could result from some other effect that is independent of any KM initiative.

Despite uncertainties in meaningful returns on an investment in a KM program, many companies have embraced KM methods, using a variety of unconventional methods of assessing outcomes. This move parallels the general trend in corporate computing, where companies invest in information technologies despite the fact that conventional metrics fail to show an eventual improvement in the bottom line. With these factors in mind, consider the continuing events at Custom Gene Factory (CGF) regarding its adventure with Knowledge Management.

Defending the Investment

Nine months into the pilot program to index, archive, and disseminate the information collected in the electronic whiteboard sessions in CGF's research and development (R&D) department, the chief knowledge office (CKO) is pressed by senior management to determine if the pilot program should be expanded to other departments or dropped. With the start of the fiscal year only three months away, the CKO is under pressure to show a return for the resources invested thus far.

The CKO is convinced that the program is making a positive contribution to the corporation. During the pilot period, he has observed an increased use of the content management system, and the corporate archive has grown from nothing to tens of megabytes. In addition, based on informal interviews, the CKO has noted an increase in overall job satisfaction in knowledge workers in the R&D department. However, neither of these measures affects the ROI calculation that could help make a case for expanding the KM initiative to include other departments.

Before making a case to senior management, the CKO explores a benchmarking approach, comparing the pilot program with other R&D departments in similar industries experimenting with Knowledge Management. However, in searching for best practices in other biotech firms, the CKO runs into confidentiality and privacy issues, given the competitiveness of the industry. As a result, the best he can do is compare practices in the R&D department with those in other departments in the corporation. Although he runs into political resistance in several departments, he manages to collect information on relative numbers of knowledge workers who regularly take part in community of practice meetings.

Unsatisfied with the positive but unconvincing results of the benchmarking effort, the CKO decides to use a balanced scorecard technique to organize the information that he will present to senior management. As illustrated in Exhibit 7.2, the technique provides a template for listing the corporation's objectives, indicators, and metrics from financial, nonfinancial, corporate, customer, and long-term and short-term perspectives.

Using the scorecard technique, the CKO associates each perspective with objectives, indicators, and metrics. For example, from the corporate perspective, the CKO's choice of indicators of change attributable to the KM initiative include quantitative, objective measures, such as cost

EXHIBIT 7.2

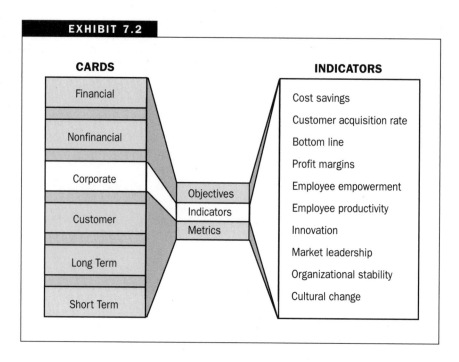

savings and profit margins, as well as qualitative, subjective measures, such as innovation, market leadership, and cultural change. Similarly, for each of these indicators, the CKO assigns metrics and corporate objectives. For example, the metric he selects for cost savings is dollars saved per quarter, and he uses employee turnover rate to quantify the metric of organizational stability. The objectives associated with each item in the scorecard are time-limited and quantified as much as possible. In CGF, the CKO's objectives for cost savings is $100,000 per year, and the objective for turnover rate is to decrease the current rate by 10 percent.

The advantage of the balanced scorecard approach is that, like formulating an RFP, a scorecard serves to crystallize management's expectations of vendors, of the CKO, and of the corporate vision. After senior management spends several weeks adjusting the indicators, metrics, and objectives so that they agree with the project trajectory they opt to expand the KM initiative to include sales, marketing, production, and customer support.

Issues

The experience of CGF's CKO in rationalizing continued investment in KM highlights several issues:

- A successful KM implementation typically requires a significant investment in people, processes, time, and technology.

- In assessing the value of a KM initiative, traditional ROI calculations and benchmarks are usually inadequate.

- It's difficult to show a return on investment for KM practices in part because of the difficulty in quantifying the contribution of enabling information technologies.

- Short-term measures of the effect of a KM initiative are generally subjective and qualitative; long-term, objective, and quantitative effects may not be measurable for years into the project.

- Techniques such as the balanced scorecard, while imperfect, provide a condensed view of qualitative and quantitative objectives, metrics, and indicators that management can use to establish the value of a KM project to the corporation.

Stakeholders

A prerequisite to understanding the economics of Knowledge Management is to define the typical stakeholders in a corporation in the midst of a KM initiative. As illustrated in Exhibit 7.3, the primary stakeholders are management, knowledge workers, and customers. The secondary stakeholders are investors, the competition, government, and outside services. The significance of each stakeholder is described in more detail next.

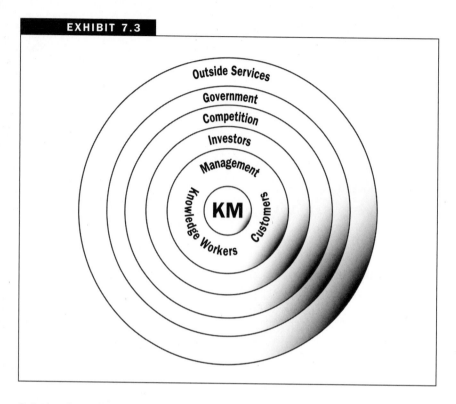

EXHIBIT 7.3

Primary Stakeholders

The value of Knowledge Management to the primary stakeholders—management, knowledge workers, and customers—depends on the perspective of the individual stakeholders. For knowledge workers, the value is in being empowered to serve customers more readily and completely and to interact more meaningfully with other knowledge workers. Knowledge workers, whether front line, knowledge engineers, or knowledge analysts, have much to gain—and lose—at the start of a KM initiative. As negative stakeholders, knowledge workers can be replaced with technologies that enable fewer people to perform their jobs more effectively and efficiently. In other words, one possible reward for contributing individual knowledge to the organization, whether in the form of rules, heuristics, or flow charts of processes and procedures, is to be downsized.

One value of a KM initiative to individual knowledge workers is an opportunity to learn in structured, corporate-sponsored seminars or formal university courses as well as in unstructured group meetings and communities of practice. An added benefit is that their value in the open labor market is usually enhanced. In most cases, the increased value and empowerment of knowledge workers overshadows the plight of knowledge workers who find themselves downsized.

The value of a KM initiative to management includes the ability to retain knowledge in the organization, more efficient and effective knowledge worker education, increased competitiveness in the marketplace, and improved profitability. However, when the number of employees involved in the downsizing is significant, organized labor frequently becomes involved. In some cases, preexisting organized labor contracts may limit the rate and degree of downsizing. These contracts may force the corporation to retain knowledge workers and distribute them to other locations in the corporation where they can be retrained and absorbed or downsized when the time limit expires.

Among management, the CIO and CKO typically have much at stake in every KM initiative. For example, the CKO's position may be contingent on demonstrable success within a few months of implementation; that is, she must be able to show that funds spent on the KM effort contribute significantly to the value of the company. Also, the CIO's workload and budget may increase significantly if the information services department is charged with creating a new infrastructure and maintaining a new suite of software tools. Because of this increased responsibility, the CIO may acquire a larger budget and more personnel.

The third primary stakeholder in the modern knowledge organization is the customer, who potentially benefits from increased quality, decreased price, or faster response from the corporation. The result should be increased customer satisfaction.

Secondary Stakeholders

The value of a KM initiative to secondary stakeholders—the investors, the competition, the government, and outside services—may not be as direct as it is to the primary stakeholders, but it can be just as great. For example, the value of a KM initiative, to investors of all sizes, from the board of directors to knowledge workers with stock options and retirement plans, can be profound if it affects the corporation's bottom line.

The value of a KM initiative to the competition depends on its success or failure. Although the competition may welcome the failure of the initiative, it can gain from a successful initiative, in that it can learn what KM approaches work in its industry.

The government also gains in that it receives revenue from sales activity of products and services as well as any increase in corporate valuation. Every business operation involves the government as a third partner. Corporations must abide by government regulations regarding everything from employee pay to termination procedures, working conditions, and payment of taxes.

Various outside services pertain directly to the KM aspects of the business and have a stake in a KM initiative. These include consulting firms, equipment manufacturers, computer hardware and software vendors, and training companies.

TIPS & TECHNIQUES

Recognition for Sharing

To encourage sharing of best practices in serving its large copiers, Xerox established a formal peer review system. Service technicians eagerly exchange their best practices, which are published company-wide, for official recognition from their peers and senior management.

Value Assessment

As the story of Custom Gene Factory illustrates, the challenge in putting a value on a Knowledge Management initiative is that traditional value measures don't reflect many of the advantages ascribed to such a program. For example, current rules for financial statements specify that intangible assets such as brand names and copyrights are recorded as assets only when they are purchased from another company, not when they are created internally. The relationship among ROI, benchmarking, and balanced scorecard methods of assessing the value of a KM initiative are explored here.

Why Not Return on Investment?

Return on investment, the tool most commonly used to evaluate business performance in terms of earnings returned on a capital investment, is a generic concept that is calculated as:

$$ROI = Return/Capital\ Invested$$

Where "Return" is the profit, income, or gain, and "Capital Invested" is the amount of capital invested during a specified period to produce the return.

The major capital investments in a KM implementation—people, processes, technologies, and infrastructure—appear in the denominator of the ROI equation. People-related KM investments employ management, knowledge workers, consultants, programming, training, and sales. Process-related KM investments include reengineering, back-end functions, and license arrangements, while technology-related investments include hardware, software, maintenance, security, and customization. Similarly, infrastructure investments include network hardware and software, facilities, and communications.

While capital investments are straightforward, the challenge in an ROI calculation is quantifying the numerator, or "Return," value because of the lack of quantitative results, especially in the short term. Innovation, corporate culture change, and market leadership aren't readily or meaningfully expressed in quantitative terms.

Benchmarking

Benchmarking, using industry- or company-wide best practices as the basis for comparison, addresses many of the qualitative limitations of ROI calculations in establishing the value of a KM initiative. In a sense, benchmarking is part of every business operation, in that corporate operations are constantly being compared with what successful companies do and earn, and managers want to increase the competitiveness of their organization by learning what other companies are doing. The main limitation of benchmarking in establishing the value of Knowledge Management or other business practice is that there may not be enough hard evidence to link the initiatives of successful companies with their current or future success. For example, in the 1990s, major consulting firms were touting reengineering as a means of excelling in business. As a result, thousands of companies engaged in some form of reengineering effort. However, although they followed the recommendations of the consultants and gurus of reengineering, the companies failed to see the promised results. If a particular company used benchmarking to assess the value of reengineering activities, it may have scored perfectly against the current benchmarks, which would have given the false impression that it was on the path to increased value. However, as it turned out, reengineering is flawed.

Similarly, given the wide range of activities that fall under the rubric of Knowledge Management, no one company is recognized as a standard worthy of benchmarking by other companies. However, pockets of activity within companies appear worthy of emulation. The challenge is to identify which company to use as a benchmark.

Balanced Scorecard

Both ROI and benchmarking are lagging indicators, in that they evaluate what happened in the past. These assessment methods provide feedback on past performance, not on how to improve future performance. In contrast, as illustrated in the story of CGF, the balance scorecard technique explicitly establishes objectives, metrics, and indicators. It establishes quantitative and qualitative objectives and how they will be evaluated. The advantage of this approach is that knowledge workers and managers all know what is expected of them to reach the objectives.

The major limitation of the balanced scorecard approach is that the objectives, metrics, and indicators are defined locally and can vary significantly from one corporation or division of the company to another. The CKO or other manager in charge of establishing metrics and indicators could pick the wrong indicators, or too many indicators, or fail to define relevant metrics. For example, in assessing the corporate scorecard, an indicator might be identified as cultural change, with a metric of the number of communities of practice in the corporation. The objective might be to, say, double the number of communities of practice in the corporation within a year. However, whether the number of communities of practice is the best metric of cultural change is debatable. The metric could as easily be the number of interdepartmental e-mail messages, and the objective could be to quadruple the number of such messages per month by the end of the first year of implementation.

Perhaps the greatest value of the balanced scorecard approach to establishing corporate value is that it provides a formal mechanism for recording corporate objectives. Like the request for proposal (RFP), the objectives component of a balanced scorecard serves as a communications

Evaluating the Value of Communities of Practice

Although the term "community of practice" is relatively new, the concept is centuries old, dating back to the guilds of the Middle Ages. The difference is the relative focus on the sharing of knowledge. For example, the guilds were created primarily to provide a monopoly for member artisans and to eliminate competition within the guilds. The sharing of knowledge was a fringe benefit that probably helped maintain the institution for centuries. In contrast, communities of practice are established primarily to share knowledge among members. The contribution of the communities of practice to the overall competitiveness of each knowledge worker in the corporation is a fringe benefit for both the knowledge worker and the employer.

Organizations that actively support communities of practice as part of a larger Knowledge Management program include Hewlett-Packard, Shell, the World Bank, American Management Systems, IBM, the U.S. Veterans Administration, and DaimlerChrysler. Each organization uses a variety of methods to foster the creation and maintenance of these communities. For example, Shell interviews each community of practice member and then publishes their stories internally in newsletters and reports as incentives for workers to contribute intellectual assets to the corporation.

tool that management and knowledge workers can use to clarify a vision of what the company needs to grow in competitiveness.

Time Value

Any assessment of the value of a KM initiative should consider the time value of investments. Like tangible assets, intangibles have a finite life span. However, unlike a building or piece of major equipment, the life span of intangible assets is much more volatile and depends on the corporate environment, employee turnover, and the market.

Consider the value of educating a knowledge worker. As discussed in Chapter 3, part of the challenge of determining the ROI for knowledge worker education includes individual differences, the finite shelf life of knowledge, lost opportunity cost, knowledge worker turnover, and the shifting marketplace. Focusing on the finite shelf life of knowledge, the relationship between corporate value and the investment in training is illustrated in Exhibit 7.4. After the initial investment in education or training, which includes tuition, transportation, time away from work, and distraction from the company's business, the value of the knowledge worker to the organization increases to some maximum value and then decays to near pre-education levels. As the exhibit illustrates, there is a break-even point for the investment in education for each knowledge worker. This point is a function of the nature of the education, the knowledge worker's salary, and fluctuations in the demand for knowledge workers with specific skills.

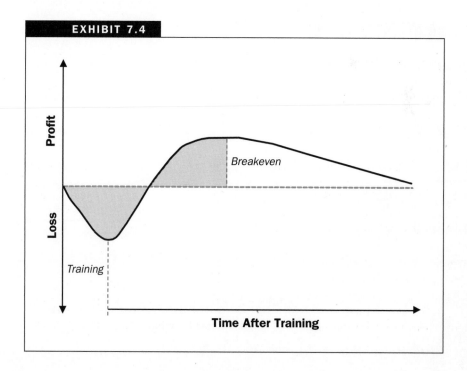

EXHIBIT 7.4

In some instances, the break-even point for resources invested in a knowledge worker may come several years after training. If a corporation invests years of knowledge worker time in training, and the person leaves the corporation voluntarily or is downsized within a few months, the corporation may not be able to recoup its investment. For this reason, corporations typically attempt to limit an early exodus of trained employees by imposing a payback penalty on outside courses taken and paid for by the corporation. However, penalties for leaving a company after in-house training are rarely imposed.

Another possibility is that there may never be a break-even point because of changes in the value of the training or because the cost of training is out of proportion to the potential benefit, as in Exhibit 7.5. Sending a manager or knowledge worker to a management course at Harvard or Stanford instead of to a local community college may increase the value of the person sent for training, but the expense may

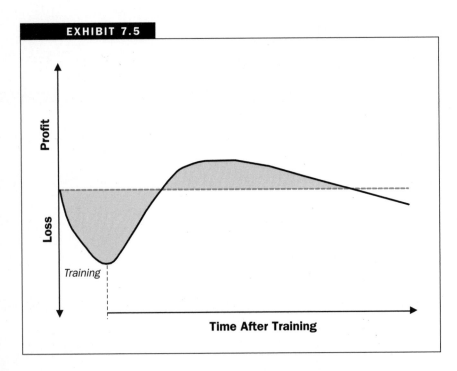

EXHIBIT 7.5

not be reflected in profit to the corporation. Furthermore, the value of the education to the corporation may be further eroded if the training was in a now-defunct technology or process. For example, at the height of the dot-com boom, hundreds of companies sent anyone who could use a keyboard to training for programming and web design. Many of the same companies found themselves downsizing these employees in a matter of months. What's more, Web programmers who once could command significant salaries and stock options found themselves unable to find a job, despite their training.

Incremental Value

One way to assess the value of a Knowledge Management initiative is to look at the incremental value of information along the KM life cycle. As illustrated in Exhibit 7.6, the contribution of the KM process to the incremental value of information varies with the processing of information. In general, the largest contribution to value is the initial creation and acquisition of information. Also significant is the translation and repurposing phase of the life cycle, in that the incremental value of translating information can result in an increase in value similar to that of the original creation and acquisition phase. Archiving, modification, and implementing user authentication and other methods of providing restricted access to the information generally provide significantly less incremental value to the information. For example, the value of information in an archive may drop precipitously because of changes in the market or within the corporation.

In addition to fluctuations in the value of information over time, there are differences in incremental contributions to the value due to administrative costs, competing services, economies of scale, inefficiencies of processing, labor costs, overhead, and the details of the process. For example, some processes, such as archiving, incur greater administrative

EXHIBIT 7.6

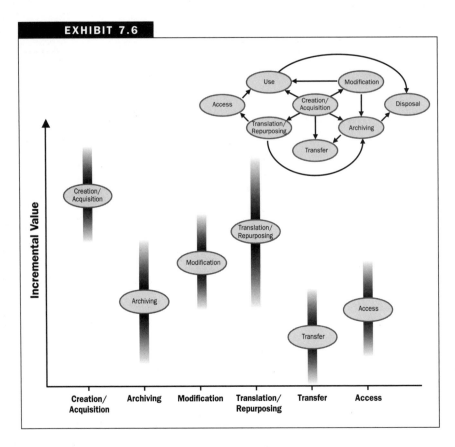

costs than others do. Similarly, competing services create an upper boundary on the incremental value of a given phase of the knowledge life cycle. For example, the cost of an outside archiving service limits the value that an internal archiving effort can add to the information.

Summary

The bottom line in assessing the value of Knowledge Management is whether it can provide significant, measurable return on the corporation's investment. In the absence of industry-wide proof that a KM approach is economically rewarding, and since ROI and benchmarking techniques cannot provide meaningful assessments, the balanced scorecard can be used to assess value and plan for future activity. However, the balanced scorecard technique is fraught with uncertainties resulting from the variability in how indicators, metrics, and objectives are assigned. Finally, when dealing with intellectual capital, issues such as information life span and time value of information have to be considered.

A little knowledge that acts is worth more than much knowledge that is idle.

—**Kahil Gibran**

CHAPTER 8

Getting There

After reading this chapter you will be able to

- Recognize the internal predictors of a successful Knowledge Management initiative

- Develop a practical Knowledge Management implementation plan

- Appreciate and recognize the risks involved in Knowledge Management

- Appreciate the significance of proper timing in implementing a Knowledge Management initiative

- Predict the likely future of the Knowledge Management industry and how it will affect your organization

Moving from theory to practice in the Knowledge Management (KM) arena requires leadership, clearly defined business goals, a receptive corporate culture, and an understanding of when and where to incorporate enabling information technologies. This chapter describes an implementation strategy that should be just as applicable to a small business as to a Fortune 500 company.

For the Record

The progression of activities in the story of how the Custom Gene Factory eventually transforms itself into a knowledge organization is indicative of the typical circuitous path to Knowledge Management. For example, in an effort to gain a competitive edge over Healthcare Productions, the management of Medical Multimedia hires a consultant to develop a multimedia asset management system. This system is designed to keep track of images, sounds, and other media that the company repackages for various customers. In creating this system, the consultant interviews company employees to determine the current process. She then designs a database system that mirrors and improves on the manual handling of multimedia assets.

In the course of the consultant's work with the multimedia, she discovers that Medical Multimedia's management sorely needs a system to track its other intellectual property as well. After a year of effort, which includes working closely with the information systems department, the consultant develops a limited KM system for tracking and managing intellectual property at Medical Multimedia. A competing company doesn't embrace Knowledge Management and succumbs to the more competitive Medical Multimedia.

Unfortunately, this early success in Knowledge Management is costly for Medical Multimedia in terms of employee relations. Most employees resist being interviewed regarding exactly *how* they perform their jobs, and one employee—the top graphic artist—leaves the company to run her own business. To minimize any further loss of intellectual capital, the consultant, working together with the head of human resources and the CEO, develops a company policy that recognizes employee contributions with public approbation as well as pay bonuses and stock options.

Meanwhile, the owners of Medial Multimedia decide to sell the company while it's at the top of the market. Since they know that the market value of the company is greater than what the books suggest, they have the consultant arrange for an independent knowledge audit.

After assessing the intangible assets in the company, the valuation is double the company's original book value, compared to previous assessments based on tangible assets alone. A biotech firm, Custom Gene Factory, acquires the company.

Custom Gene Factory's CEO, who is impressed by the usefulness and value of the knowledge audit, hires a chief knowledge officer (CKO) who reports directly to the chief information officer (CIO). The original KM consultant, demoted by CGF, resigns and offers her services to the company as a high-priced consultant.

The strategy for KM initiatives in the company is now in the hands of the CKO. After observing the ad hoc communities of practice that have formed in CGF, he proposes a computer-based collaborative system for key knowledge workers and senior managers. His plan is accepted, and, after several months of work, an electronic whiteboard system that supports instant collaboration is in place and in use. With the success of the electronic whiteboard system under his belt, the CKO proposes a corporate-wide strategy for indexing, archiving, and disseminating the information recorded by the electronic whiteboard.

Working closely with a team of senior managers, middle managers, and representatives from various communities of practice, the CKO crafts a request for proposal (RFP). This document reflects the corporate consensus on the technical capabilities that are needed to facilitate Knowledge Management. After an extensive evaluation of the solutions available, including an assessment of the vendors and developers, a vendor is selected, and a contract is negotiated for a pilot project in the company's research and development (R&D) division.

About a year into the pilot, the CKO is faced with the challenge of defending spending on the KM system to move it company-wide. Because ROI and benchmarking tools fail to capture the benefits and goals of the KM project, the CKO uses a balanced scorecard technique to convince senior management to opt for company-wide expansion of the KM system. What remains to be seen is how the system will be accepted by the company's knowledge workers and how the investment in corporate resources will be reflected in corporate value—which is where the leadership of the CEO and other senior managers comes into play.

Issues

Custom Gene Factory's circuitous path from a multimedia asset management system to a corporate-wide KM system, which includes acquisition of Medical Multimedi and several internal initiatives, highlights many of the issues relevant to a practical KM implementation:

- A successful implementation requires a solid plan that makes provision for multiple contingencies and the leadership to bring the plan to fruition.

- A KM implementation plan should include a strategy for achieving employee buy-in, including a means of shifting corporate culture from one of knowledge sequestering to one of knowledge sharing.

- The focus of a KM initiative should reflect both the perceived needs and ad hoc experiences of knowledge workers and management. That is, a formal KM initiative should amplify current KM practices, regardless of how latent.

- A knowledge audit can provide quantifiable valuation of intangible corporate assets. When applied appropriately, this technique has a proven track record of delivering value to the corporation.

- Knowledge engineers, knowledge workers, and KM consultants work synergistically with others in the corporation. Similarly, the CKO typically reports to the CIO or other senior manager.

- Loss of intellectual capital, in the form of attrition of knowledge workers and management, is a part of everyday business and a primary reason for implementing a KM system capable of archiving and repurposing rules and heuristics.

- Realistic implementation time lines for KM initiatives range from several months for limited, department-wide projects to a year or more for corporate-wide systems.

- Perhaps the greatest challenge of KM professionals is proving to investors, senior management, and other primary stakeholders that transforming the corporation into a learning organization through KM methods will result in a significant, quantifiable increase in corporate value.

Implementation Overview

A successful Knowledge Management implementation requires that senior management understand the corporation's needs and have a clear vision for its future, a grasp of the range of technologies available for enabling the KM processes that apply to the corporation's business, and the experience to navigate the inevitable legal, contractual, and economic hurdles ahead. Addressing these requirements systematically through an established process maximizes the odds of success and provides senior management with flexibility in modifying the approach to meet their needs.

The road map offered here, consisting of five major phases, addresses practical a KM implementation from the perspective of senior management aided by a CKO or KM consultant:

1. *Ad hoc experience.* Collect data about the company's ongoing KM activities.

2. *Fact finding.* Determine if a corporate-directed KM implementation is warranted and feasible.

3. *Formalize approach.* Define specific milestones and outcomes for success.

4. *Implement.* Take action.

5. *Evaluate.* Assess progress toward milestones and outcomes, and, based on the results of the evaluation, follow one of the four following paths:

>   **a.** *Modify.* If the current solution doesn't suit the needs of the corporation, then modify the approach and implement a new KM solution. Since few implementations will work perfectly on the first attempt, this is the most likely initial outcome of the evaluation phase.

>   **b.** *Extend.* If the KM solution suits the needs of the corporation, either from the initial attempt or as the result of a modified approach, then extend the solution through more of the corporation.

>   **c.** *Maintain.* At some point, the corporation will reach a steady-state condition in which the current KM solution is stable and satisfies the corporation's foreseeable needs. Maintenance of a KM system is a dynamic process that will require a continual stream of resources.

>   **d.** *Disable.* If the current approach to Knowledge Management fails, at some point senior management has to decide whether to continue to invest resources in it or to disable the current implementation process and either reformulate the strategy or wait for changes in technology or corporate culture.

Ad Hoc Experience

The first phase of the implementation process involves observing the internal processes of the corporation as they relate to Knowledge Management. Even if there isn't a formal KM process in place, virtually every corporation is involved in KM activities. Everyone in business creates, archives, repurposes, transmits, shares, copies, modifies, and disposes of information on a daily basis. What may be missing is a formalized approach to extending the practice—which may be personal or limited to a small working group—department- or corporate-wide.

Fact Finding

The second phase of a KM implementation process involves a systematic information-gathering initiative that extends and builds upon the ad hoc experiences within the organization and extends to factors external to the corporation. The major fact-finding activities revolve around five key axes:

1. Stakeholders
2. Strategy
3. Finances
4. Corporate culture
5. Tactics

Questions and issues relevant to each of these axes are provided.

Stakeholders. Early in the implementation process, it's important to clarify who is for and who is against a KM initiative. In creating a map of the political landscape, including primary stakeholders, it's also key to identify any hidden agendas. Are there any major dissenters in senior management? If so, is the resistance surmountable? Similarly, will there likely be resistance from organized labor? Finally, in working with stakeholders, who should have a say in deciding on the details of the implementation approach?

Strategy. Strategically, it's key to identify the problems that proponents of the KM initiative hope to solve. In particular, why is a KM initiative preferable to other strategies? What are the projections for the growth of the company, the industry, and the need for Knowledge Management? How well will a KM project fit with the overall corporate strategy?

Another issue is how Knowledge Management will likely affect the company's core competency. For example, if the company enjoys technological superiority in an area, how will a KM implementation leverage this advantage?

Finances. The financial feasibility of moving to a knowledge organization depends on projections for the company's future needs and whether addressing these needs warrants investment in a KM initiative. As with

TIPS & TECHNIQUES

Timing Is Everything

Implementing a Knowledge Management program takes time and requires the coordinated timing of events. Relevant questions to ask before making the move are:

- What is the motivation to change?
- Is the current business process viable without a KM program? If so, then why change?
- Is there a consensus at all levels in the organization that a KM program is necessary?
- Is the corporate culture ready for change? If not, what is necessary, other than the simple passage of time, to prepare it for change?
- Is there a commitment to long-term support from senior management?
- What are the risks of changing—and not changing—now?

A KM program not only costs the corporation money and other resources, but also increases or at least changes the nature of the workload of virtually every employee. Instead of simply responding to situations, employees may have to respond and then take the time to document their decision-making process. Although the burden is greatest at the start of a KM program, the overhead never completely returns to the original baseline level.

all business endeavors, timing is critical, especially relative to planned mergers and acquisitions. Developing a KM system, unlike developing a comprehensive information system, can't simply be outsourced to an external vendor. It involves integration of processes, cultural change, and technology within the corporation. What's more, a KM implementation can take years and involve significant investments in training and in information technology.

Corporate Culture. In exploring the financial feasibility of a KM implementation, due diligence on the part of management includes exploring options from outsourcing to using internal development staff. Decisions on how to handle development will determine the short- and long-term capital requirements as well as the scope of the planned implementation and how disruptive it will be to the corporate culture. For example, if the company prides itself on its close relationship with employees, then a significant downsizing associated with a KM initiative may be unacceptably disruptive to the corporate culture —especially if resources that could have been used to pay employees in the company instead go to outside vendors.

Other issues that affect corporate culture include the interest, at all levels in the organization, of formalizing ad hoc KM behavior into a KM system. Because a move to Knowledge Management and the associated technology infrastructure represents a major shift in employee skill set requirements, some employees may resist the move for fear of being downsized. Corporate stability also may be adversely affected if employees opt to find employment elsewhere instead of submitting to the overhead of documenting their activities and decisions.

Tactics. Hundreds of unknowns need to be addressed. For example, are there sufficient in-house resources to create a KM system? Is the time line for implementation reasonable and compatible with other corporate activities? How will privacy and security concerns be addressed? How will quality control be implemented? What additional training will be required for employees and management, and at what direct and indirect cost? Similarly, of the hundreds of enabling technology solutions, which are most appropriate and affordable?

Exactly how internal fact finding is carried out depends on the culture and size of the corporation. For example, external fact finding through site visits can help facilitate external data gathering and provide the implementation team with a perspective on exactly what is involved day-to-day in an implementation effort. Sending a corporate representative to attend seminars, networking with colleagues in other businesses, and working with consultants also can facilitate external fact finding. Regardless of the approach used, for implementation to move past the fact-finding phase into a formalized approach, senior management must be fully behind the initiative. This is true whether the motivation for a KM implementation is to increase profitability, to provide higher-quality service, or to transform the corporation into a learning organization.

Formalize the Approach

The third phase of the Knowledge Management implementation process involves formalizing the approach—that is, developing a comprehensive plan—based on ad hoc experiences and the results of fact-finding. One of the key tools at this phase of implementation is the request for proposal, which documents much of the internal strategic planning. For example, the RFP defines the functional and requirements specifications for any technologies involved in the implementation. These include definitions of the operational constraints of technology, such as hardware and software requirements, in terms of performance and standards.

A formalized approach includes details on project management, including resource management, time lines for technology infrastructure improvements, contingencies for problem management, slips in time lines, and disaster recovery. Perhaps the most important issue during this phase of implementation is expectation management, as expressed in return on investment and customer service. In this regard, a clear definition of the metrics for success is key to helping direct the flow of resources over the implementation of the KM system.

Implement

The fourth phase of the implementation process involves taking action and actually doing the work defined in the implementation plan. Working the plan normally involves vendor selection and negotiating contractual agreements, such as legally binding agreements between vendors and the corporation. If external vendors are involved in development, such as information system infrastructure development, a variety of service-level agreements may be involved as well. The human resources department typically is intimately involved in this phase of implementation, especially if extensive downsizing, training, and recruiting of employees are in store.

Evaluate

The fifth major phase of the implementation process is evaluating the results of the efforts in the first four phases. A component of the evaluation phase is problem management, in that there are inevitably problems in timing, cost overruns, and the way resources are managed. For example, service-level agreements may have to be modified to reflect the reality of what vendors actually can deliver.

Evaluation is a continuous process that involves reexamining internally monitored metrics as well as service-level agreements with outside service providers at regular intervals and adjusting the implementation processes accordingly. Rarely can a KM system be established on the first attempt. For example, a pilot program may be evaluated and the decision made that it must be modified before it can be extended throughout the organization. In other cases, the problems discovered during the evaluation phase may be insurmountable, and the entire program may need to be discarded.

A major milestone in the evaluation phase is signing off on work that has been performed internally and by vendors. However, even if everyone involved with the project has delivered within specifications and according to agreements, the resulting KM system may not work as expected. In most cases, the approach will have to be modified to reflect the results of the evaluation. For example, a videoconferencing system may not work as expected because of interruptions and delays in audio and video signals. The service provided by the DSL or cable modem vendor doesn't provide sufficient bandwidth for uninterrupted audio and video conversations to be held over the Internet. Knowledge workers and managers may be forced to use a cumbersome telephone conferencing system for the audio portion of the conversation and the Internet for the video segment. As a result, setting up an impromptu meeting via the Internet may be practically impossible, and knowledge workers may opt to use telephone conferencing. The modification in this example might be to purchase a higher-end videoconferencing system that includes special hardware for compressing the audio and video in real time so that conference participants can see and hear each other in real time.

Risk Management

For most senior managers, managing risk is a continuous process that involves rethinking strategies and employing tactics to maximize likelihood of success. One of the primary tactics for managing the risks associated with a KM implementation is learning to predict where threats can arise and to recognize threats as soon as possible. As described here, the key areas of risk associated with a KM initiative relate to:

- Management
- Politics
- Finance
- Law
- Technology
- Marketing

Management

The implementation activities associated with risk range from selecting an appropriate implementation strategy, establishing a workable reward system, and filling resource requirements, to dealing with excessive market volatility, maintaining focus, exercising the appropriate leadership, and selecting the appropriate vendors. For example, in selecting the best implementation strategy, management must decide whether to attempt a corporate-wide implementation from the start or to experiment with a limited pilot program.

The advantage of a pilot program is that there is limited risk in the event that the project fails, less financial exposure, and less disruption of the corporate culture. There's also the advantage of being able to select the department or division most likely to be receptive to the change. Doing this maximizes the odds of success because the successful experience serves as an illustration to others in the company of the advantages of embracing Knowledge Management.

Politics

Virtually every KM initiative involves the challenge of navigating through a maze of internal corporate politics. For example, powerful internal stakeholders may find it in their best interest to quash a KM initiative because it threatens their control of information, which they

IN THE REAL WORLD

Achieving Buy-in

Access to timely information is the limiting factor in real-time decision making. As part of a Knowledge Management program in a major teaching hospital in the Northeast, the administration decided to provide emergency room clinicians with PC-based voice recognition systems to replace the traditional dictation service. Unlike the manual transcription service, which provided a two-day turn-around time, the voice recognition system promised virtually real-time data entry into the hospital's computer system. Although the system seemed to make sense to the administration, they failed to adequately consider the clinicians involved in the implementation.

From the clinicians' perspective, the effect of the voice recognition data entry system was to shift the burden of transcription from the dictation staff to them. What's more, there was no reward for participating in the time-intensive practice of carefully dictating into the voice recognition system and then editing the transcribed information before submitting it to the hospital information system. As a result, a year after the implementation of the system, it was used only occasionally by curious clinicians who rotated through the emergency room.

The situation turned around when the hospital administration worked with clinicians to explain the potential cost savings to the hospital from real-time monitoring of clinical activity and savings on manual transcription fees. In a compromise move, the administration agreed to pay clinicians $5 per transcribed record, or between $75 and $100 per day, to use the system. Compliance rose from near zero to about 80 percent over the course of a few months. Clinicians still prefer to use the traditional transcription service when rushed for time, but most are willing to use the voice recognition system because they perceive it as an activity that is recognized, valued, and rewarded by the hospital administration.

may view as a source of their power. The R&D head may not want managers in other departments or even senior management to be able to instantly review his department's progress on a particular project. Similarly, the CIO may view a CKO who reports directly to the CEO as a threat. If so, it may be in the CIO's best interest for a KM initiative that isn't controlled by information services to fail.

Dealing successfully with internal politics involves performing a stakeholder analysis early on in the project and addressing problem areas before they surface. For example, if the CIO is seen as a possible impediment, the CKO should form an alliance with him or her. The CKO should involve the CIO in all major decisions and make it clear to the other senior managers that the CIO is taking responsibility for the technology component of the project. In this way, the CIO is motivated to do whatever it takes to make the KM implementation a success.

Finances

The financial risks of a KM implementation are numerous. They range from accounting questions, known and unknown competition, the general economic environment, the appropriate infrastructure investments, and forming strategic partnerships. It is important for management to deal successfully with the time pressure and the prospect of lost opportunity costs.

Financial risks can be addressed by judiciously choosing strategic partners and by investing incrementally in infrastructure, in a way that minimally penalizes future expansion. For example, it's generally better to invest in a slightly more expensive network infrastructure that is scalable rather than a less expensive solution that supports current needs but would have to be replaced when KM activities were expanded. Many hardware vendors cater to this conservative approach to infrastructure development by offering devices that can be expanded by the addition of plug-in hard drives, processors, and memory, as dictated by demand. Similarly, many software vendors offer solutions (and licenses) that scale robustly with the number of processors available. Obviously, financial decisions based on the underlying technology should involve the CIO as well as the chief financial officer.

Law

The major legal risks of a KM initiative involve domestic and international intellectual property issues. For example, a corporation with foreign offices can be restricted in the degree of knowledge sharing permitted through a KM system. In addition, special U.S. tax rules apply to intellectual property used abroad. Furthermore, constantly changing laws restrict the international transfer of information. There are also unilateral organizations, free-trade unions, and bilateral treaties—such as the European Union (EU) and NAFTA (North American Free Trade Act)—that may adversely affect international contracts. Other risks include the failure of vendors and developers to honor contractual obligations and challenges from organized labor regarding the potential downsizing of employees through KM practices.

Many of the legal risks can be addressed at least partially by retaining the services of legal counsel as a cost of doing business. A company that has significant dealings with overseas vendors or overseas offices should have both domestic and internal legal counsel review all major contractual and employment agreements.

Technology

The technology-related risks of a KM initiative, like the financial risks, often seem pervasive. The major risks are associated with standards, scalability of the solutions selected, security, and, ultimately, the usability of the KM system. For example, even if the vendor and developers seem to be the most appropriate for the job at the time of implementation, it's possible that industry standards will suddenly shift, resulting in significant reworking costs or a dead-end system.

Marketing

Internal marketing risks primarily involve the unreasonable expectations of middle management and knowledge workers. It's tempting to oversell a solution to achieve buy-in, but the downside is that the users may have unrealistic expectations that the Knowledge Management system will never meet. These and related internal marketing risks are usually best addressed by involving representatives for all internal stakeholders at every step along the way to full implementation. In this way, the representatives can communicate realistic expectations to intended users before the system is brought online.

Predictors of Success

Effective leadership is a predictor of a successful Knowledge Management initiative. Positive predictors of success include a CEO and other senior managers committed to creating a knowledge organization who can clearly articulate a vision for the company, are competent in KM techniques, and are experienced with change management.

Second on the tier of positive predictors is a motivated, capable workforce composed largely of knowledge workers who recognize the potential benefits of Knowledge Management. The operational excellence of the corporation is also important, to the degree that the organizational structure can facilitate KM activities through outcomes measures, such as the use of benchmarks and balanced scorecards. A related predictor is the availability of the appropriate infrastructure technologies, including provision for voice and data communications and the requisite hardware and software platforms that support KM-specific tools. Of course, a modicum of luck is always necessary for success, where luck is defined as the intersection of preparedness, opportunity, strong economy, significant business growth potential, and a clearly defined market.

Future

The future of Knowledge Management is tied to improvements in information technology and the accumulation of hard evidence that Knowledge Management positively and significantly improves the bottom line in specific industries. Knowledge Management can operate independently of technology. However, the increased pervasiveness of information technology at home and in the office indirectly minimizes the cultural change hurdles associated with every KM initiative.

For example, a few years ago, personal digital assistants (PDAs) were limited to the technophiles and deep-pocketed business professionals. Today, most employees (and high school students) are comfortable with entering their contact information and calendars on PDAs in the interest of saving time. Similarly, e-mail has become an indispensable enabler in the office environment, providing asynchronous communications and thereby freeing knowledge workers from the endless loop of voice mail messages. As information technology permeates the fabric of the corporation, Knowledge Management will one day cease to be considered a separate entity or activity; like e-mail, it will become an expected part of the workload.

Of course, until that time, corporations keenly invested in securing an advantage over the competition will embrace differentiating technologies at the leading edge of Knowledge Management. For example, some forward-looking companies are investigating the potential of the Great Global Grid (GGG) to support real-time information visualization and expert systems as components of hand-held decision support systems. The GGG promises to bring supercomputer power to knowledge workers through their PDAs.

Another KM-related technology on the near horizon is virtual Knowledge Management, where the wired and wireless web enables knowledge workers to collaborate and communicate, regardless of location. Of course, there are concomitant issues of security, privacy, and the inability of knowledge workers to escape work in a fully connected world. Despite these challenges, Knowledge Management, like a fully computerized corporation, remains an increasingly achievable goal that is quickly becoming expected corporate behavior. The challenge in most organizations for the CEO and other senior managers is to make a judicious commitment to explore the potential of a KM strategy in their unique environment.

Summary

Knowledge Management begins with a practical implementation plan that adequately addresses people, process, and technology challenges, whether working with vendors and developers or shifting the corporate culture to embrace the concept and reality of a knowledge organization. An insightful and capable senior manager can recognize and appreciate predictors of a successful KM initiative and manage the potential risks involved. As long as stakeholder expectations are managed in a way that avoids the hype that kills other business innovations, the prospects for a successful KM implementation, and for the KM industry as a whole, look exceptionally bright.

> *The great danger for most of us is not that our aim is too high and we miss it, but that it is too low and we reach it.*
>
> **—Michelangelo**

Further Reading

Books

Harvard Business Review on Organizational Learning. (2001). Boston: Harvard Business School Press.

Hamper, B. (1991). *Rivethead: Tales from the Assembly Line.* New York: Warner Books.

Horibe, F. (1999). *Managing Knowledge Workers.* Etobicoke, Ontario: John Wiley & Sons Canada Limited.

Hruby, F. (1999). *TechnoLeverage.* New York: AMACOM Books.

Martin, J. (1996). *Cybercorp.* New York: AMACOM Books.

Michaels, E., H. Handfield-Jones, et al. (2001). *The War for Talent.* Cambridge, MA: Harvard Business School Press.

Rumizen, M. (2001). *The Complete Idiot's Guide to Knowledge Management.* New York: Alpha Books.

Shortliffe, E., L. Perreault, et al., eds. (2001). *Medical Informatics: Computer Applications in Health Care and Biomedicine.* New York: Springer.

Tiwana, A. (1999). *The Knowledge Management Toolkit: Practical Techniques for Building a Knowledge Management System.* Englewood Cliffs, NJ: Prentice-Hall.

Weneger, E. (1987). *Artificial Intelligence and Tutoring Systems.* New York: Morgan Kaufmann Publishers.

Periodicals

CIO Magazine

Knowledge Management Magazine

MIT Sloan Management Review

Harvard Business Review

Web Sites Catering to Knowledge Management

American Productivity & Quality Center: *www.apqc.org*

CIO Magazine's Knowledge Management Research Center: *www.cio.com/research/knowledge*

Knowledge Management in the Federal Government: *www.km.gov*

Knowledge Management Magazine: www.kmmagazine.com

Online: www.onlinemag.net

Virtual Business Magazine: www.vbmagazine.com

Wharton Business School: *www.Knowledge.Wharton.upenn.edu*

Glossary

American Productivity and Quality Center (APQC) One of the leading industry groups in the area of Knowledge Management. APOC is credited with kick-starting the application of Knowledge Management in business.

Application A software program that supports a specific task, such as word processing.

Application service provider (ASP) A technology that provides access to software through a Web browser, negating the need for the customer to purchase and run the software locally.

Architecture The general technical layout of a computer system.

Artificial intelligence (AI) The branch of computer science concerned with enabling computers to simulate human intelligence. Machine learning, natural language processing, neural networks, and expert systems are all examples of applied artificial intelligence.

B2E management Business-to-employee management, where the knowledge worker is treated like a customer to certain business services.

Back-end process A process that doesn't represent a company's unique skills, knowledge, or processes. Typical back-end processes include payroll, billing, and accounts payable. A back-end process moved to a shared services unit becomes the core competency of the unit.

Balanced scorecard A measurement method used to assess the value of a Knowledge Management initiative, based on a balanced view of short- and long-term objectives, financial and no financial measures, lagging and leading indicators, and internal and external perspectives.

Bandwidth A measure of the information-carrying capacity of a medium. On the Internet, bandwidth is commonly measured in bits per second.

Benchmarking A method of comparing contract services to services delivered.

Best practice The most effective and desirable method of carrying out a function or process.

Biometrics Means of verifying user identity, based on unique individual characteristics, such as fingerprints and retinal patterns.

Bot Short for "software robot." In the context of an emotionally intelligent interface, a displayed representation of a person whose actions are based on programming.

Brainstorming The process in which one or more knowledge workers focus on a problem and the deliberately come up with as many unusual solutions as possible.

Browser A software program that interprets documents on the web. Netscape Navigator and Microsoft Explorer are the two most popular browsers in use today.

Cable modem A high-speed (large-bandwidth) device for accessing the Internet. Cable modems and DSL represent the most popular, affordable means for customers to gain high-speed Internet access.

Capital expenditure An expenditure on tangible and intangible assets that will benefit more than one year of account.

Chat The instantaneous exchange of text messages between two or more participants. Chat is like e-mail without the delay.

Client-server A computer architecture in which the workload is split between desktop PCs or hand-held wireless devices (clients) and more powerful or higher-capacity computers (servers) that are connected via a network such as the Internet.

Cluster analysis One of several computationally efficient techniques that can be used to identify patterns and relationships in large amounts of customer data.

Community of practice A group whose members regularly engage in sharing and learning, based on common interests.

Content management Oversight of the creation, submission, quality assurance workflow, versioning, and auditing of knowledge assets.

Contract A binding agreement made between two or more parties that is enforceable at law.

Controlled vocabulary A terminology system unambiguously mapped to concepts.

Core competency The skills and processes that distinguish a company from the competition, typically based on the company's ability to build a dominant set of technologies and skills that enable it to adapt to quickly changing marketplace opportunities.

Customer relationship management (CRM) The dynamic process of managing a customer-company relationship such that customers elect to continue mutually beneficial commercial exchanges and are dissuaded from participating in exchanges that are unprofitable to the company.

Data mart An organized, searchable database system, organized according to the user's likely needs. Compared to a data warehouse, a data mart has a narrower focus on data that is specific to a particular work group or task.

Data mining The process of extracting meaningful relationships from usually very large quantities of seemingly unrelated data.

Data repository A database acting as an information storage facility, usually without analysis or querying functionality.

Data warehouse A central database, frequently very large, that can provide authorized users with access to all of a company's information. A data warehouse usually is provided with data from a variety of noncompatible sources.

Database Management System (DBMS) A system to store, process, and manage data in a systematic way.

Decision support system Software tools that allow managers and other knowledge workers to make decisions by reviewing and manipulating data in a data warehouse.

Digital subscriber line (DSL) A type of high-speed Internet connection based on the same copper wiring used for standard telephone service.

Disruptive technology A technology that empowers a different group of users and gets better over time. The PC is a disruptive technology, in that it empowered individuals to perform tasks once relegated to large data centers.

Downsizing Reduction in employee headcount.

Early adopter In marketing circles, a customer who wants the latest and greatest gadget, regardless of cost or inconvenience.

Ease of learning Regarding a user interface, the ease with which a particular interface can be learned. Contrast with **ease of use**.

Ease of use Regarding a user interface, the ease or efficiency with which the interface can be used. An easy-to-use interface may be difficult to learn and vice versa.

Economic Darwinism Survival of the fittest, most economically successful companies in the marketplace.

Economies of scale Reduction in the costs of production due to increasing production capacity.

E-learning The use of the web, intranets, wireless computing, and other digital means of teaching and learning at home and in the workplace.

Electronic data interchange (EDI) A standard transmission format for business information sent from one computer to another.

Employee relationship management (ERM) A dynamic process of managing the relationship between knowledge worker and corporation such that knowledge workers elect to continue a mutually beneficial exchange of intellectual assets for compensation in a way that provides value to the corporation and are dissuaded from participating in activities that are unprofitable to the corporation.

Encryption The process of encoding data to prevent someone without the proper key from understanding the data, even though they may have access to it.

Enterprise resource planning (ERP) The category of software designed to improve the internal processes of a company.

Expert system A type of computer program that makes decisions or solves problems in a particular field, by using knowledge and analytical rules defined by experts in the field.

Forecasting A mathematical method of extrapolating historical performance data to aid in planning.

Frequently asked questions (FAQs) Lists of questions and their answers, often posted on a web site for users with questions of their own.

Functional specifications The technical document that specifies exactly what a software and/or hardware system will deliver.

Gantt chart A graphical production scheduling method showing various production stages and how long each stage should take.

Genetic algorithms Algorithms that are designed to mutate, breed, and spawn new, more fit algorithms, based on their success in solving a particular problem.

Great Global Grid (GGG) The next-generation web, which provides access to processing power and software resources on demand.

Heuristic A rule of thumb. Expert system knowledge bases commonly contain a great many heuristics.

Infrastructure In the context of information technology, the system of servers, cables, and other hardware, together with the software that ties it together, for the purpose of supporting the operation of devices on a network.

Intellectual property Know-how, trade secrets, copyrights, patents, trademarks, and service marks.

Internalization The process of matching the content in a web site to suit the language and culture of specific customers.

Internet *An* internet is a collection of local area networks (LANs) connected by a wide area network (WAN). *The* Internet is the World Wide Web, one of many internets.

Knowledge audit A formal evaluation of the value of knowledge assets in the company.

Knowledge engineering The process of extracting knowledge from an expert with enough detail and completeness that the knowledge can be imparted to others or to an information system.

Knowledge management A variety of general and specific technologies for knowledge collection (e.g., data mining, text summarizing, the use of intelligent agents, and a variety of information retrieval methodologies), knowledge storage and retrieval (e.g., knowledge bases and information repositories), and knowledge dissemination and application (e.g., intranets and internets, groupware, decision support tools, and collaborative systems).

Knowledge organization An organization that creates, acquires, transfers, and retains information.

Knowledge repository A central locations of information on best practices

Knowledge workers Employees hired primarily for what they know.

Knowledge base A database that contains information about other data contained in the database. The data or information needn't reside in a traditional database management system to be considered a knowledge base.

Lagging indicator An outcome measurement.

Leading indicator A predictive measurement.

Legacy system An existing information system in which a company already has invested considerable time and money. Legacy systems usually present major integration problems when new, potentially incompatible systems are introduced.

Localization The process of adapting content to a particular country or region.

Lost opportunity cost The cost of not applying resources to toward an alternative investment.

Loyalty A positive inner feeling or emotional bond between a customer and a business or a brand. Loyalty can't be assessed directly but can be inferred from a customer's actions.

Loyalty effect The quantifiable behavior normally associated with loyalty, such as repeatedly transacting business with a particular retailer or web site.

Machine learning Software systems that operate through some degree of self-programming. Machine learning is an area of study in the field of artificial intelligence.

Metadata Data about data: how the structures and calculation rules are stored, information on data sources, definitions, quality, transformations, date of last update, and user access privileges.

Natural language processing (NLP) A system of parsing text for machine recognition purposes.

Network hardware The cables, routers, bridges, firewalls, and software that enable computers to connect to shared printers, databases, and each other.

Object oriented A system based on independent, self-contained program or data structures that are hierarchically related.

Ontology A formal, explicit specification of a shared concept that forms the basis for communications.

Operations The analysis of problems associated with operating a business, designed to provide a scientific basis for decision making.

Optical character recognition (OCR) A technology that automatically converts text printed on paper into machine-readable text that can be incorporated into a computer system.

Overhead The expense of running the business as opposed to the direct costs of personnel and materials used to produce the end result. Typical overhead costs include heat, rent, telephone, computers, and other office equipment.

Personal digital assistant (PDA) A personal, hand-held organizer. The Palm Pilot is the quintessential PDA.

Personalization The process of modifying content to suit the needs and preferences of a particular user.

Process management An evaluation and restructuring of system functions to make certain processes are carried out in the most efficient and economical way.

Process map A graphic description of a process, showing the sequence of process tasks, that is developed for a specific purpose and from a selected viewpoint.

Process optimization The removal or reengineering of processes that don't add significant value to a product or service, impede time to market, or result in suboptimal quality.

Reengineering The process of analyzing, modeling, and streamlining internal processes so that a company can deliver better-quality products and services.

Request for proposal (RFP) A document that requests prospective service providers to propose the term, conditions, and other elements of an agreement to deliver specified services.

Requirements specifications A description, in operational terms, of what management expects the vendor's product or service to do for the company.

Residual value The value remaining in a device as a function of time. The longer the time from the original purchase date, the lower the residual value.

Return on assets (ROA) The ratio of operating earnings to net operating assets. The ROA is a test of whether a business is earning enough to cover its cost of capital

Return on equity (ROE) The ratio of net income to the owner's equity. The ROE is a measure of the return on investment for an owner's equity capital invested in the shared services unit.

Return on investment (ROI) Profit resulting from investing in a company, process, or activity. The profit could be money, time savings, or other positive result.

Rule-based expert system A type of expert system that uses a knowledge base composed of IF-THEN clauses as the basis for its reasoning.

Sales force automation (SFA) The use of software and other technologies and processes to facilitate the sales process.

Server A computer that controls access to the network and net-based resources.

Service-level agreement (SLA) An agreement between the parent corporation or other customer and the shared services unit in which the unit agrees to provide services to a specified performance level.

Slack In the context of project management, the time in which a minor process or activity can be completed in advance of the next major operation or activity that depends on it.

Social capital The sum of the resources embedded within, available through, and derived from the network of relationships possessed by an individual or social unit.

Software escrow An arrangement in which a software developer places the source code for its applications in the hands of a third party that will make the source code available to a customer in the event that the developer fails. Software escrow gives the customer the option of maintaining mission-critical applications on its own.

Statistical process control A benchmarking method based on statistical quality control.

Strategic services Processes that directly affect a company's ability to compete.

Synergy The benefit derived from the cooperation between two business entities.

Systems integration The merging of diverse hardware, software, and communications systems into a consolidated operating unit.

Tacit knowledge Knowledge that is unspoken or implied.

Taxonomy The classification of concepts and objects into a hierarchically ordered system that indicates relationships.

Text-to-speech (TTS) Voice synthesis, using e-mail or other text source to drive the voice synthesis process. Providing an animated character with speech via TTS is more bandwidth efficient than sending voice over the Internet.

Thought processor An outline generator that has features beyond those found in a traditional word processing outline program, such as the ability to convert the outline instantly into a graphical flow diagram.

Total cost of ownership (TCO) The cost of owning a device or technology, including operating expenses.

Total quality management (TQM) A customer-centric philosophy based on constant improvement to meet customer demands.

Touch point In the context of knowledge worker relationships management, a point of contact between a company and its knowledge workers.

Value chain The sequence of events in a process that adds value to the final product or service.

Virtual knowledge management A Knowledge Management model in which knowledge workers and management work and communicate through the web and other networks.

Index